The Night Shift

Ian Newton

Published by
RPM Publications
BCM Box 3328
London WC1N 3XX
Tel: 07967 886257
E-mail: mm014y08547@blueyonder.co.uk
Website: www.red-star-research.org.uk

The characters in this book are real; you will find them in any
workplace especially at night time.

Distributed in the UK by AK Press and Distribution
PO Box 12766
Edinburgh EH8 9YE
0131 555 5165
order@akedin.demon.co.uk

ISBN: 0-9543014-5-5

THE NIGHT SHIFT

The Night Shift is a sit-com of six episodes from Ian Newton, author of the best-selling 'Dustbingate'. It is about the hard and gritty world of working people, this particular world being that of the night shift.

It is based on Ian's own experience of working permanent night shifts in various factories in the Hull area. The particular appeal of 'The Night Shift', however, is that it will be a familiar world for any who have been in this situation; readers and viewers will identify with the characters that Ian has created.

'The Night Shift' is essentially about the bar room philosophers and barrack room lawyers who can put the world to rights on the back of a fag packet and still have room to make a note of the next days favourite in the 2.30 at Epsom. It is about making mischief and having a bit of a laugh so that the long hours of a seemingly interminable shift become endurable

The world of the night shift worker is a strange place (as anyone who has worked there will know); it breeds its own special characters who find the darkness (and the absence of bosses!) an excuse to have some fun at the company's expense. Life is one big wind up or one long laugh from the start to the end of the shift.

As there are some people in Hull who might recognise themselves in the scripts (and to protect the publisher from slander or compensation claims!) names have been changed to protect the guilty.

The publisher is sure that once this book is published there will be a massive crackdown on the theft of toilet rolls, light bulbs and the odd cement mixer on Night Shifts across the country!

'The Night Shift' is Ian's third book and, in many ways, his best.

The main Characters:

Night shift manager: Fat Jeff

Quality Controller: Raghead

Quality assistant: Malcolm

Process Worker: Monkey Hanger (he hates Hartlepool)

Process Worker: Big Gus

Process Worker: Black Dave

Process Worker: Harry

Fork lift truck driver: Mary (a man)

IAN NEWTON

Ian Newton was born in Hull in 1950 of English and Yemeni parents. He spent most of his childhood on the streets of Hull's deprived Hessle Road district. Ian was a factory fodder kid who went to a factory fodder school; factory fodder was expected to be the peak of his ambition.

Defying these expectations, Ian was determined to become a writer and in the course of his struggle to achieve this he has had a thousand and one jobs ranging from factory labourer to industrial chemist; Ian is currently at Hull University completing a degree in Social Work.

It was to fulfil his dream of becoming a chronicler of working-class life that Ian endured the 1001 indignities that is an intrinsic part of working-class experience; it is this experience that gives his writing such vitality and relevance.

After a number of false starts, Ian burst onto the scene in 1998 with a book that created a media sensation and resulted in the Labour Government fearing for its very survival. 'Dustbingate' (his best selling book which was a withering attack on John Prescott and his cronies in Hull) was the launching pad for Ian's subsequent career.

Tony Hall

In a development which will give Prescott ever more sleepless nights, Ian has turned 'Dustbingate' into a film script which is being managed by Hollywood agent Joe Weiner who has purchased a two-year option on the film rights.

THE EPISODES

THE WIND UP

The scene is a typical factory canteen for night shift workers. The room is small and there is one scruffy table surrounded by an assortment of equally scruffy chairs. The table is littered with sandwich boxes, newspapers, cigarette ash and tea stains. In the corner of the canteen there is a small dirty kitchen, in another corner there is a coffee and a chocolate machine. A notice board hangs askew on the wall.

Fat Jeff, the night shift manager, is immaculately clean in his two piece blue uniform and polished white safety helmet. He has just put his money in the coffee machine.

Suddenly the sound proof door on the other side of the canteen bursts open and the sound of noisy machinery can be heard as Gus, who is absolutely black from head to foot, walks in.

Big Gus: [*Super rough voice, in panic*] Jeff! Jeff! The boiler's just blown the big valve, and Mary has just crashed his fork lift into a lorry's diesel tank. There's diesel all over the yard.

Fat Jeff: Oh bloody hell Gus! Look what you've made me do. I've pressed the wrong button now and that's my last twenty pence.

[*Coming through the same sound proof door Mary, the night shift fork lift truck driver, is being hotly pursued by a big angry lorry driver. Mary is also black and filthy from head to foot. The two are arguing.*]

Driver: Well I'm not bleedin' cleaning it up. And who's going to pay for the damage?

Mary: [*Smooth, calm effeminate voice*] Well I most certainly am not. If you had parked where I told you to park it wouldn't have happened, you stupid buffoon.

Driver: Ere! Who are you calling a baboon? If you want a face like Jack Pallance, then you just keep talking.

Mary: [*Moving towards Fat Jeff, his voice indignant*] Jeff, did you hear that? This driver has just abused me.

Fat Jeff: [*Who is still engrossed in the coffee machine and the loss of his twenty pence*] You haven't got twenty pence on you Mary?

Mary: [*Voice more indignant*] I said this man has just abused me.

Driver: I never touched ya. Ya lying woofta.

Mary: [*Effeminately angry*] Did you hear that Jeff, he called me a woofta.

Fat Jeff: [*To the driver*] Eh, now there'll be less of that type of talk. We have all sorts of people working here. Some are black, some are brown and some are puffs. It is one of my jobs to protect my staff from attitudes like yours. I will bend over backwards for this man.

Big Gus: Well if that isn't an offer Mary, I've never heard one.

Fat Jeff: Now if I hear that sort of talk again, I'll have no alternative but to ban you from the site.

Driver: [*Growling*]: You do that mate and I'll have you. I'll wait for you, and when I get you I'll tear your head off, break both your legs and tie 'em in a knot round ya big fat neck.

Mary: [*Goading Jeff*] Go on Jeff, stick one on him!

[*The driver is looking fiercely at Jeff. Jeff swallows hard and smiles nervously. He takes Mary to one side.*]

Fat Jeff: [*Discretely to Mary*] I think what's called for here is some diplomatic management skill.

Mary: Just what I was thinking.

[*Fat Jeff goes back to the driver*]

Fat Jeff: Now as I see it, we have a choice here. One of you is at fault. As a manager it us up to me, as it were, to give the judgement of Solomon.

Driver: Just a minute. Who's this Solomon?

Fat Jeff: [*Smiling*] The wise king who took his sword out to cut the child in half.

Driver: [*Sceptical*] That was Jack the Ripper.

Mary: [*Interrupting*] Wrong! He killed ladies of the night.

Big Gus: [*From across the canteen*] I thought that was Crippen.

Mary: No, he was the wife poisoner.

Driver: [*Thoughtfully*] Didn't he do the Wombles in the 80's?

[Through the other door Raghead, the quality controller and his helper, Malcolm come from the laboratory next door. Raghead is immaculately clean, whilst Malcolm is black from head to foot]

Raghead: [*Yawning*]: What's all the noise about in here, has someone made a cup of tea without informing the science department?

Fat Jeff: You haven't got twenty pence have you Raghead?

Raghead: No, but Malcolm has. Give him twenty pence Malcolm and then put the kettle on. My mouth feels like a camel's scrotum.

Malcolm: [*Mumbling as he gives Fat Jeff the twenty pence*] Smells like one.

Raghead: Just put the kettle on Malcolm and keep your insidious mumblings to yourself. Just remember, any more quick-fire quips like that and you could wear out one of the two brain cells that you have left. That would qualify you for night manager. What would Jeff do then eh? [*He walks over to the table and sits down next to Gus*]

Fat Jeff: Er you want to watch it Raghead. There's people upstairs got their eye on you. There's rumours you've been fiddling your quality reports. In fact I think one's just been nominated for the Booker Prize of fiction.

Raghead: I could sue for talk like that.

3

Malcolm: [*Sitting down at the table*] I thought ya could only sue people when what they were saying wasn't true?

Raghead: [*Sneering*] Just go and make the tea Malcolm and try to stop your brain moving your mouth.

[*Malcolm indignantly gets up again and goes to make the tea*]

Big Gus: Ere, Raghead who was that infamous doctor who went round poisoning wives? The driver says it was Jack the Ripper. I think it was Crippen. But Mary says he cut women up.

Driver: [*Pointing to Fat Jeff*] And he said it was Solomon.

[*Fat Jeff gets his coffee and goes to sit down next to Raghead and Gus at the table*]

Raghead: [*Looking at Fat Jeff*] Educated guess eh Jeff? I had no idea you were a religious man. Did this come to you revelation like? A blinding bolt from God one night while cooking the production figures. This could be another biblical breakthrough on the Holy Scriptures. I can see the headlines now in the Sun. 'Night Shift manager blows the lid off scriptures. King Solomon was really Jack the Ripper.'

In fact if you think about it that's how he might have escaped after the murders. There he is old Solomon the Ripper out for a fun night in some foggy London dockland, picks up a couple of old Sheba's, next thing you know it's back to his place in the Chariot for a bit of a slap and slash. And here comes the clever bit, the reason they could never catch him. He escaped by parting the waters of the Thames.

A very interesting theory that Jeff. I'll have to put it to the Rabbi next time I see him in the Kosher butchers.

[*Malcolm returns to the table carrying a massive dirty teapot and sits down with the others*]

Malcolm: Nah, you're both wrong it wasn't Solomon who parted the waters, it was Noah after a message from God.

Mary: Don't be stupid Malcolm, Noah built a boat to escape the great flood.

Malcolm: [*He starts to pour out the tea into the waiting mugs*] Oh yeah, that's right. I knew it was something to do with water.

Raghead: You mean just like what you've got on the brain.

Malcolm: [*Thoughtfully*] Who was the one who parted the waters then?

Driver: I remember now, wannit that black bloke with the bald head. Wots his name now? Ah it's right on the tip of my tongue.

Fat Jeff: Oh I know who you mean, Gandhi.

Driver: Nah not him, he was a Pakistani.

Fat Jeff: Well he was a black bloke with a bald head.

Driver: Well it wasn't him. Anyway he didn't have bald head. His head was shaved.

Fat Jeff: He was still bald.

Driver: Yeah but this bloke was really bald with alapeaches.

Malcolm: My dad went bald during the war. My mum said it was through the shock.

Mary: [*Understanding voice*] Oh you mean the horrors of war eh Malcolm. I suppose that's understandable.

Malcolm: No it was a letter. One of them brown letters from the Government. Mum said after he read it he never stopped crying for days.

Mary: [*Understanding voice*] Yes a lot of people got letters like that. Terrible. One his family was it, killed in action?

Malcolm: Nah, they were his call up papers. Dad thought he'd fooled em ya see. A couple of months earlier before when they'd tried to get him, he wrote back telling them he had one leg.

Jeff: Just a minute they called up your dad when he had only one leg?

5

Malcolm: Nah he had two.

[*Jeff looks at Raghead*]

Raghead: Don't worry, we'll get there in the end.

Big Gus: [*Baffled*] If your dad had two legs, why did he tell them he only had one? I mean it's not the type of thing a doctor's gonna overlook is it.

Driver: Not unless he's like my doctor. He's Indian wiv a turban. Nice bloke mind but can't understand a bleedin' word he says. Last time I went to see him, he told me he thought I was malingering.

Mary: That's not very nice is it. What did you say?

Driver: Told him din I. Told him no matter what I did I couldn't keep warm.

Jeff: Sounds serious. What did he give you for that then?

Driver: Nufink. The biryani ballbag sold me a red anorak and pair of jeans for £14.99.

Raghead: That's not a bad price. Those anoraks, does he do them in blue?

Driver: Nah, I asked him about that. Only had red, said he'd sold clean outa blue. Red dunt suit me, our lass ses wiv me blood pressure I look like a post box if I go out in it.

[*From the back of the canteen Harry, Monkey Hanger and Black Dave come into the canteen. They are all black from head to foot*]

Jeff: Oh here they come. Sleep walking again.

Raghead: Some of us have actually been busy tonight, Monkey Hanger. Someone had to push back the borders of science whilst the nation sleeps.

Harry: Oh yeah and how many years have you pushed them back now? You must be somewhere near to 1066 by now.

[*They all take a seat round the table and Monkey Hanger starts to pour himself a cup of tea. And out comes the hand rolling tobacco*]

Harry: [*Big smiles*] You've found out where the day staff hid mucky books then?

Raghead: [*Big smile*] Hundreds of glossy little female nubiles just waiting to be ogled at. And guess where we found them…..the M.D's office. His desk was full of them. The man's a pervert.

Fat Jeff: Oh my God, not the M.D's office. You lot are gonna get me sacked. He was bloody fuming last time one of you lot used the shower in there and smudged a great big Mars bar onto the hand towel.

Raghead: Don't worry Jeff. We'll put the door back on its' hinges later on.

Harry: Well wiv all them mucky mags lying around Malcolm won't have to use his imagination anymore when he sneaks off for one of those nocturnal trips to the bog.

Malcolm: [*Flushed and embarrassed*] I don't know what you mean. I only go to the bogs when I have to. I've always been regular.

Monkey Hanger: Oh come off it Malcolm. You must be the only bloke who can have a crap with his boots pointing towards the wall.

Driver: [*Suddenly interrupts*] Yule Brynner!!

Harry: Where?

Driver: No. That bald dark bloke who parted the waters.

Black Dave: Talking of things that part. I think I'll just go and take a look at those mucky books.

[*Black Dave gets up and lecherously slinks from the table into the lab next door*]

Raghead: That wasn't Yule Brynner, that was Charlton Heston.

Driver: No it wasn't, it was Yule Brynner, because I can remember he put his magic stick on the waters and it all changed to a shit brown colour.

Harry: [*Cringing as he sips his tea*] He hasn't made this tea an'all has he?

Raghead: [*Adamant, argues back*] No!! If you remember Yule Brynner was the Egyptian King. Charlton Heston had been shagging his bird before he married her, but he blew her out to help the yid slaves, and she said she would stiff him if he ever darkened her throne again.

Monkey Hanger: This sounds like an invigorating conversation.

Driver: [*Pointing to Fat Jeff*]: Well he started it. He said Solomon was Jack the Ripper.

Monkey Hanger: Just a minute, have I missed something here?

Mary: No he never. Gus said that. It was me who said that he killed ladies of the night.

Gus: [*Argumentative*] No, I didn't!! I said it was Crippen.

Harry: Where the bleedin hell does Crippen come into all of this!!

Gus: He's the one who cut up all them women in the olden days.

Malcolm: [*Suddenly singing gives a little dance*] Remember you're a Womble!!

[*Everybody stares at him*]

Harry: Feel better now that you've got that out ya system?

Malcolm: No Crippen. Didn't he do the Wombles?

Driver: That's what I said.

Harry: Sorry to disappoint you, but I don't think he murdered the Wombles.

[*Black Dave comes back carrying an armful of dirty magazines*]

Harry: Now if anybody will know, our resident pervert will. Dave, who was that who used to murder all them women in the olden days?

[*Dave slams down the pile of magazines onto the canteen table in triumph*]

Black Dave: Ah that ones easy. Sweeney Tood wannit.

Monkey Hanger: No! Sweeney Todd was a barber.

Raghead: Well who did he kill then?

Monkey Hanger: Anybody I suppose.

Big Gus: You're all wrong, it was Crippen.

Black Dave: What, him that did the Wombles?

[*Across the table Mary starts to get his bait out. He has a jar of pickled onions and some sandwiches*]

Raghead: Actually I think Dave's right. It was Sweeney Todd. He used to get his customers in for a short back and sides and in between the friendly patter to get them off their guard he used to slit their throats.

Big Gus: He wasn't very clever then was he! Surely his regulars in the waiting room must have noticed him carving up the customers in between a shampoo and a shave.

Raghead: Well that's where you're wrong see. He didn't have any regulars 'cause he killed them all.

Malcolm: Well how did he make a living if he killed all his customers?

Raghead: 'Cause he was clever that's how. He wasn't just a barber. He used to make and mix his own shampoo and soaps, then sell it to the nobs.

Malcolm: Oh right, a bit like Vidal Sassoon ya mean.

Harry: The only difference is that Vidal Sassoon rips you off, and Sweeney Todd rips you up.

Raghead: Yeah, that's right. Old Sweeney gave a whole new meaning to the words 'Wash and go'.

9

Monkey Hanger: Eye man and remember that in those days barbers were allowed to do surgery and practice medicine. That's how he used to earn most of his living between carving up people as a hobby like.

Driver: One of the old school of medicine eh, kill or cure.

Fat Jeff: [*Serious voice*] My, strange world innit. I wonder what turns a respected member of society into a murderous, lunging throat slasher.

[*Harry lurches across the table at Fat Jeff. His eyes glaring madness at him*]

Harry: [*Scary*] Who knows what madness lies at the darkest recesses of the human mind. The brain can harbour a stinking, slimy cesspit of perverted crazed intent towards the innocent. Who knows Jeff, you might be talking to any one of us in all innocence. Next minute you're laid in a crumpled bloody heap, coughing up your large intestine.

Fat Jeff: By heck, you'ra a right happy sod tonight.

Harry: I'm just saying, that's all. Ya shouldn't go upsetting people needlessly. Especially on a night shift.

[*Harry pauses and pulls a folded piece of paper from his overalls and throws it to Jeff*]

Harry: Just sign us me overtime sheet Jeff.

Driver: Did they ever catch this Sweeney bloke then?

Monkey Hanger: No man, went on working for years before they finally caught up with him. And it was by pure chance. Apparently ol Sweeney was heavily into necrophilia, bestiality and sadism. In that day and age, with so little socialising and stuff, he was flogging a dead horse. Anyway one day he joined this ancient club for gentlemen. Called the Hell Fire Club.

Malcolm: The Hell Fire Club?

Monkey Hangar: Yeah, ya know the type of place, drinking, bonking till all hours, maybe a bit of whipping thrown in just to spice the atmosphere a bit.

Black Dave: Hey, this sounds my type of place. Is it still open?

Driver: Yeah there's one in town called the Pink Elephant.

Raghead: No, that's a bleeding gay club, the Pink Elephant.

Fat Jeff: Oh I know where you mean. Just past the bus station. It's the one with great pink doors with an elephant painted on it.

Driver: That's the one.

Fat Jeff: Inside they've got those swing type cages you can dance in. [*Laughing*] Makes you real dizzy. If you go upstairs you can get chicken nuggets or scampi in a basket.....

[*Fat Jeff's voice slowly begins to fade as he realises everybody is watching him. His voice suddenly changes, all abashed*]

Fat Jeff: A friend of mine told me about it. It's quite violent these days. There's been a lot of stabbings.

[*All eyes are on Jeff. The driver and Monkey Hanger move away their chairs a touch. Mary smiles at him*]

Malcolm: Go on then Monkey Hanger, how did they catch him?

Monkey Hanger: Well the story goes that one day whilst he was at the club he was found in one of the back rooms sticking pins in his testicles.

[*Mary has just got a pickled onion on the end of a fork, ready to eat*]

Mary: [*Mumbling*] Don't think I'll bother.

Malcolm: Bleedin' hell, sticking pins in ya ball bag!

Monkey Hanger: Why eye man, don't knock what you've never tried. Apparently it's still practised by some remote tribes in Africa. In fact many experts believe that's why so many of our black friends are so well hung downstairs.

Malcolm: [*Inquisitive*] What, makes it bigger like?

11

Monkey Hangar: Ooooooh eye man. The Encyclopaedia Britannica reckons it can put two inches on your snake. If ya don't believe us ask Dave there.

Malcolm: Is that right then Dave?

Black Dave: [*Joining in the wind-up*] You betcha man. My granddad swears by it, and he's eighty and still cleaning my gran's chimney.

Monkey Hanger: That's right. Medical experts today say it can enhance sexual pleasure up to six times and give ya the staying power of a Peruvian mountain donkey.

Malcolm: Get-away

Monkey Hanger: No it's true man. Ya see old Sweeny was a pervert ahead of his time. Who knows what he'd have been if he'd been alive today.

Monkey Hanger: They still use Sweeney's methods in all these modern sex clinics.

Raghead: It's called nacupuncture.

Malcolm: Nacupuncture?

Monkey Hanger: Its Chinese for pinball.

Malcolm: Oh yeah, I think I've heard of it. The Chinese use it a lot don't they. Clever lot them Chinese.

Monkey Hanger: Aye and it's the biggest nation on earth remember man. Shagging is their national sport. They're at it all the time.

Harry: Haven't you ever wondered why ya can never see them cooking ya meal when ya go for a Chinese takeaway… [*Pause*]

Monkey Hanger: Exactly! 'cause there at it like a load of rabbits over ya pork balls mate.

Malcolm: [*Interest aroused*] Do you er… do you need, eh special needles for this like?

Monkey Hanger: No man! Sweeney Todd used his rusty darning

12

needles. In fact in his memoirs Sweeney ses to get the full benefits of his therapy the bigger the needle the better

Malcolm: [*Strangely losing interest, stands up*] Well ere…..I think I'll just go tidy up in the lab then.

Raghead: [*Knowingly*] No, no Malcolm you sit down mate. Get your feet up. I'll tidy up later.

Malcolm: [*Insisting*] No it's alright I'll do it. You know me, I always like to keep my hands on me job.

[*He moves steadily towards the door, and disappears into the lab next door. Monkey Hanger, Raghead and Harry look with smiles at each other*]

Monkey Hanger: Is there any, erm, needles in there then ?

Raghead: [*Raghead mischievously nods*] In the cupboard with the squeaky door.

[*We hear the loud squeak of a creaky cupboard door opening*]

Driver: What happened after they caught him in this room then?

Monkey Hanger: Who?

Driver: Sweeney Todd.

Monkey Hanger: Oh him. Well what would any respectable pervert do when they found out one of their members had sunk to a new level of depravity without letting his mates in on the secret. Naturally they felt hurt didn't they. I mean what type of mate's that!

Driver: That's not a mate is it?

Monkey Hanger: Anyway he was brought before the club committee, to answer for his sins as it were. But despite desperate pleading and putting forward yet another innovative perversion to try and curry favour, namely sucking dirty feet, the committee wouldn't have it. It wouldn't wash.

Driver: What, his feet?

Monkey Hanger: No, his story. After that memorable meeting of the Hell Fire Club committee, which all committed perverts remember as historic, old Sweeney was kicked out.

Driver: They blackballed him then?

Monkey Hanger: Well they might have done before they threw him out, I'm not sure.

Fat Jeff: Come off it Monkey Hanger. What a load of old bollocks. You're winding us up.

Driver: What happened to him after that then?

Monkey Hanger: [*Eyes glaring, fiercely whispering*] Nothing was ever heard. Legend and myth has it, Sweeney took a job as a pathologist at a local hospital. As far as I can remember he was hung not long after for carrying out an incorrect procedure on a female patient during one of his post mortems.

Driver: Bit strong innit, hanging him just for that.

Fat Jeff: [*Sceptical*] Go on then. What was this incorrect procedure then?

Monkey Hanger: She was alive.

Fat Jeff: [*Laughing*] Getaway

Monkey Hanger: No, no, I tell you no lies. Despite a plea of mitigation the trial judge expressed his suspicion that it was not normal practice for post mortems to be carried out at three in the morning in an east London cemetery with a cavalry sword and a garrotte.

[*Suddenly there is an almighty scream from outside the canteen. It sounds like Malcolm*]

Driver: What the hell was that then!!

Raghead: That's Sweeney come for Jeff for mocking him.

Fat Jeff: [*Suddenly windy*] Go have a look Mary.

Mary: Sod off! You go, I'll back you up.

14

Harry: [*Joking*] That's two directions you'll have to watch Jeff.

[*A few seconds later and Malcolm comes running into the canteen, trousers round his ankles. He is wearing a pair of loosely fitting Y fronts, and holding his crutch. He is dancing around in agony*]

Driver: Hey is he some sort of nutter or what?

Mary: Oh my God!! He's possessed!

Driver: I bet it's Sweeney!

[*Fat Jeff in a panic gets out of his chair and crosses his hands in the sign of a cross*]

Fat Jeff: Be gone you fiend!!

Harry: What's up wiv ya Mal, no bog roll again?

[*Malcolm is still rushing around holding his crutch in agony*]

Malcolm: I missed and stabbed meself in the fireman's helmet. It's still in there and it's killing me.

Fat Jeff: This is all your fault Monkey Hanger, putting ideas into his head. Come on Raghead, you're the shift first aider, you'll have to see to him.

[*Raghead gets up to assist*]

Big Gus: I hope he hasn't used a rusty needle. You'll have to suck out the poison.

[*On second thoughts Raghead sits back down*]

Raghead: I just remembered my first aid ticket's ran out.

Fat Jeff: When!!

Raghead: About two seconds ago.

Fat Jeff: [*Panicking*] Just take it easy Malcolm, Monkey Hanger you'll have to take him to hospital.

Monkey Hangar: I'm not taking him!!

Fat Jeff: Well somebody's got to take him.

Monkey Hanger: It's not the taking I'm bothered about. It's the explaining.

Fat Jeff: Gus go through and ring an ambulance.

[*Gus gets up and pushes through the sound proof door – we hear the sound of machinery — Fat Jeff goes over to Malcolm and tries to calm him*]

Fat Jeff: [*Trying to be professional*] Now calm down son. You're going to be alright son. Just take it easy.

Harry: [*To the others*] He's a goon inne.

Fat Jeff: [*Arm around Malcolm*] 'Ere, lay down here on the floor and try to relax.

Malcolm: How can I relax with a syringe needle stuck in me winky.

[*Fat Jeff gets him on the floor*]

Malcolm: [*Whimpering*] I'm cold down here Jeff.

[*Fat Jeff starts to unzip his jacket. We see the putrid expression on his face, as he gets a whiff of Malcolm's body odours, and on second thoughts zips it back up again*]

Fat Jeff: [*Big smile*] There'll be here soon son.

Raghead: I'd like to see how you write this one up in the accident log Jeff.

[*They are all sniggering. Suddenly we hear the sounds of sirens and see flashing lights on the canteen window*]

Driver: I hope he doesn't come in fast. There's half a ton of diesel oil on the floor outside.

Fat Jeff: [*Sudden horror*] O shit! I forgot about that!

[*We hear the screech of brakes, bangs and crashes. Everybody rushes to the canteen window. We hear the feeble sound of a broken ambulance siren*]

Monkey Hanger: [*Looking out of the window*] Wow! Did ya see that hand break turn?

Harry: [*Looking though the window*] What a driver! If he had just held it for a few more seconds he would have missed the boiler house.

> [*Fat Jeff quickly gets to his feet from next to where he has been holding Malcolm's head. He lets his head fall carelessly to the floor. He rushes to the canteen window and looks out*]

Fat Jeff: [*In horror*] Oh my God!! Where's the bike shed!!!!

Raghead: I think it's in the Boiler House. Hey just look at that Jeff, your mountain bike's on the roof. Well half of it is anyway.

Malcolm: [*From the floor in agony*] Raghead, is my bike alright?

Raghead: [*Looking hard*] Can't see it.

Harry: Yeah, there it is. Looks alright, is it one of them folding bikes?

Malcolm: No!

Harry: Oh well it is now.

Mary: Ooh look they're getting out. They don't look injured. Oh just a minute, one of them's fell over.

Raghead: [*Shock*]: One of them's lost his legs!!

Fat Jeff: [*Covering his eyes*] Oh I can't look.

Driver: Nah, he's a midget.

Raghead: Oh yeah.

Harry: Is that Gus down there?

Fat Jeff: If he's winding them up I'll kill them.

Monkey Hanger: Oh look at that man. The big one's got his hand round Gus's neck.

Driver: He's probably just taking his pulse, using the artery in the neck. Mr Spock did it on Star Trek.

Fat Jeff: I thought Dr Who did that?

Driver: He's not in Star Trek, is he?

Harry: Look, Gus is pointing them up here. Hey they're coming up.

Mary: Ooooooh that big one looks angry.

[A *few seconds later and the two ambulance men come into the canteen. One of them is massive. The other one is a midget. They step over Malcolm*]

Big ambulance man: [*Breathing fire*] Who's in charge here?

[*All together and in one chorus, they point to Fat Jeff and say HE IS!!*]

Big Ambulanceman: [*Near to tears*] Do you know what you've done to my ambulance… you've wrecked it. The back doors won't open, the front grille is bent, I've got two flat tyres and to top it all there's a Honda Fifty sticking to the windscreen.

Small Ambulanceman: Don't forget the woo woos Bert.

Big Ambulanceman: Of yeah and you've bust the woo woos.

[*Fat Jeff looks mystified, he looks at Harry*]

Harry: You know Jeff … [*He makes a sound like an ambulance siren*] Wooo, wooo, wooo.

Fat Jeff: Alright, alright never mind the side effects

Big Ambulanceman: Only it dun't do that anymore. It goes… [*Sad and slow*]…Wuuu… wuuu wuuu. I gonna make sure your company gets the bill for this.

[*Malcolm is still on the floor moaning*]

Small Ambulanceman: [*Looks down at Malcolm*]: What's up with him then?

Fat Jeff: He's the one who's had the accident.

Big Ambulanceman: Let's have a butcher's then. [*He kneels *down beside Malcolm. Voice now understanding*] You just take it easy son and tell me what happened.

> [*Malcolm is still on the floor curled up with his hand over his crutch*]

Malcolm: [*All pathetic*] Oh it hurts, give me some cocaine.

Big ambulanceman: Just relax now son. Let's inspect the injury site.

Driver:[*To Fat Jeff*] He's just reassuring him first that that's the way to do it. My wife works at the 'ospital. She's up on all this stuff.

Fat Jeff: Oh really, nurse is she?

Driver: Nah, cleans the shit houses, but she loves the place.

Big ambulanceman: [*Very loud voice*] What the bloody hell….? [*He looks over his shoulder towards the needle stuck in the top of Malcolm's dick*] Poooooh [*Cringing*] he dun't half hum as well. Don't you ever wash downstairs?

> [*Suddenly a message interrupts the big ambulance man's radio*]

Controller's voice: Central to seventeen, come in seventeen over.

Big ambulanceman: [*Into lapel microphone*] Seventeen receiving, over.

Controller's voice: What's the delay seventeen. Advise of injuries to patient, over.

> [*The big ambulanceman pauses, his voice is somewhat reluctant to answer*]

Big ambulanceman: He's got er……a needle stuck in his ….erm prick over.

Controller's voice: Say again seventeen. Stuck in his what? Over.

Big ambulanceman: [*Getting angry*] I said prick! Prick!!

Controller's voice: [*Indignant*] Who are you calling a prick!! Arsehole!! Over.

Big ambulanceman: [*To colleague*] Bleedin hell, what's the code for this shorty?

[*Small ambulanceman – shorty — gets the injury code book out of his top pocket and starts to look through it*]

Small ambulanceman: I'm not sure but I fink it's a forty fifty one.

Big ambulanceman: Nah, that's a beer bottle up the jacksy.

Small ambulanceman: I don't fink it's in. Oh yeah here it is. It's a forty fifty two. I was nearly right.

Monkey Hanger: Will ya look at that man, they have codes for everything.

Driver: That's clever innit.

Big ambulanceman: Oh yes we have codes for the lot. What's the code for on the spot treatment for a forty fifty two Shorty?

Small ambulanceman: [*Looks back at code book*] A sixty niner.

Harry: This should be interesting.

Big ambulanceman: Yeah, well ere. I think we'll have to take him to hospital. You get his arms Shorty, I'll gets his legs.

[*Both ambulancemen lift up Malcolm*]

Small Ambulanceman: How come I get the heavy end?

Big ambulanceman: Well you can have this end if ya want 'cause it stinks.

[*They struggle with him towards the door*]

Driver: Ere before ya go settle an argument for us.

[*The two struggling ambulancemen turn in the door frame inadvertently folding Malcolm's legs and arms together. He screams*]

Big ambulanceman: Sorry son. What's that then?

Driver: Who was it that used to cut up all them women in the olden days? I say it was Jack the Ripper.

Big ambulanceman: What's this then a quiz?

Driver: [*Pointing to Jeff*] Nah, he said it was Solomon.

Small ambulanceman: We've got a Dr Solomon at the hospital.

Driver: What about Sweeney Todd?

Small ambulanceman: Nah, he don't work there.

Big Gus: Well, I say it was Crippen.

Big ambulanceman:[*To colleague*] Come on Shorty, they're all bleeding nutters in here.

[*The two ambulancemen start again to struggle Malcolm through the canteen door. But before they go, the small ambulanceman pauses in the door frame and looks back. He has a curious look on his face*]

Small ambulance man: [*To all*] Wot, him that did the Wombles?

[*All the lads look blank as they return to the table. The flashing lights of the ambulance go past the canteen window and you can hear the most pathetic ambulance siren*]

THE PRODIGAL FATHER

Members of night crew are sitting quietly around the canteen table drinking tea and reading newspapers. As usual, apart from Fat Jeff they are all black from head to foot in their blue two-piece overalls and white safety helmets.

Fat Jeff is reading 'The Independent' newspaper, Mary 'The Times', Black Dave a pornographic magazine, Big Gus a Viz Comic, Malcolm a copy of 'Socialist Worker.' All are at peace with the world. Fat Jeff puts down his paper and sighs with contentment.

Fat Jeff: This is the life eh. Everything running smoothly. All's well with the world. Times like this I feel at one with the Universe.

Mary: [*Creeping*]: Got the finger on the pulse you see Jeff.

Fat Jeff: That's what management's all about — delegation, being in control.

Big Gus: [*Still reading his comic*] Get us a coffee Jeff.

Fat Jeff: White, no sugar Gus.

[*He gets up and walks to the coffee machine and gets Gus his coffee*]

Fat Jeff: Knowing how to give orders.

Big Dave: [*With head in a mucky magazine*]: I'll have one while you're there Jeff. A twenty-one. No sugar.

[*Fat Jeff brings the coffees back to the table*]

Mary: A man in control, that's you Jeff.

Malcolm: [*Head in paper*] Just close the door Jeff. It's bloody freezing in here.

[*Jeff gets up to the close the door*]

Fat Jeff: Management is the art of the subtle. Giving orders without letting people knows it's an order.

Big Gus: [*Still reading the paper*] While you're up just get is me bag.

[*Jeff picks up Big Gus's bag and puts it on the table*]

Fat Jeff: Never let staff take advantage Mary.

[*Big Gus collects the bag*]

Big Gus: Oh bloody hell; it's the wrong bag. Can't you do anything right?

Fat Jeff: Sorry Gus. [*Jeff takes the bag back and retrieves the right bag*] Psychology, that's the key word to management Mary. Some manager's here let the staff run them ragged.

Mary: Not you eh Jeff.

Fat Jeff: [*Sitting back down*] Phew no chance. It's not often somebody disobeys me. Put it this way, they don't do it twice Mary. Malcolm just close that window behind you [*Malcolm doesn't move from reading his copy of Socialist Worker*] Malcolm just close that window please?

[*Still no response. Without realizing Jeff gets up and closes the window*]

Big Gus: [*Head still in comic*] Leave the window open.

Fat Jeff: One other thing Mary always be consistent, when you've made a decision stick to it. It's fatal to back down. Staff will just think you're weak.

Mary: [*Creeping*] Fair but firm, that's you Jeff.

Fat Jeff: [*Flattered*] I like to think so Mary.

Mary: Here have a chocolate biscuit Jeff.

[*He offers Jeff the open packet*]

Fat Jeff: [*Sniggering*]: And why not, let's spoil ourselves eh Mary.

[*He takes a chocolate biscuit and gives it a little nibble*] Another thing Mary, and this is the golden rule. Never, I say never let your staff get away with verbal abuse. Mmmmmmmmmmmm chocolate gingers, my favourite.

Mary: [*Still creeping*] I was wondering Jeff if you had signed my holiday form for Friday night off?

Fat Jeff: Oh sorry Mary can't get cover. Everybody wants Friday night off. [*Jeff eats the rest of the biscuit*] Mmmmmmmmmmm these are nice Mary. [*He goes to take another*]

[*Mary churlishly snatches away the packet*]

Mary: Well bloody buy your own, you fat arsehole!

Malcolm: [*Still engrossed in his paper*] It says here New Labour is cracking down harder on run-away fathers.

Mary: About bloody time. I don't see why I should have to pay for other people's pleasure. My partner Courtney thinks it's a national disgrace how some men just walk out on their responsibilities leaving us tax payers to pick up the bill for the brats.

Malcolm: Yeah, you're right Mary. It's a bit like paying for a prossi and letting someone else knock her off.

Fat Jeff: Well there's another conversation straight down the sink.

Mary: No, no. In his own retarded way, Malcolm's got a point.

Big Gus: Yeah, that's right, good on ya Malc.

Malcolm: [*Flushed with pride*] Yeah, yeah, that's right I have got a point [*Sudden pause*] what is it?

Mary: Well it's obvious isn't it?

[*He waits for an answer*]

Malcolm: Well yeah…but give us a clue.

Mary: [*Dogmatically*]: Well, people should be responsible for their own actions.

Malcolm: Yeah, that's right!!!

Mary: Another thing, I reckon a lot of these so-called one-parent families have only themselves to blame. I mean a lot of the kids have a touch of tar brush.

Fat Jeff: Ey up, don't be upsetting Dave now.

Black Dave: Don't worry about me. I'm British mate. Passed the Tebbitt cricket test. But I wouldn't let Raghead hear you talking like that.

Fat Jeff: Talking of Raghead, where the bleedin' hell is he? It's not like him to miss the chance of getting his arse on a chair.

Malcolm: Where he always is at this time. Getting his head down in the women's bogs.

Fat Jeff: [*Angry*] If he's robbing that bloody tampax machine again I'll have him. You can always tell when he's been at it. Comes up here with his pockets bulging and its coffees all round. It's the only time he ever offers.

Mary: Now here's a good point in question. He's always with different women. I bet he's got a few sprogs knocking about.

[*At that precise moment Raghead enters the canteen. Big Gus jumps to his feet and slaps the table*]

Big Gus: [*Mocking child's voice*] Blocked ya. One! Two! Three! My turn to hide.

[*As usual Raghead is immaculately clean, but he has obviously been asleep. He stretches and yawns*]

[*Raghead goes over to the table and picks up the tea pot*]

Raghead: [*In shock*] It's cold!!

Fat Jeff: [*Mocking*] What a deduction. Have you ever thought of forensics as a career Raghead?

Mary: It's a wonder with all the tea you drink that you don't piss aniseed balls.

Raghead: What's this, pick on Raghead night?

Fat Jeff: [*Sniggering*] Give it, but he can't take it. What's wrong, got up out of the wrong side of the toilet?

Raghead: Ah sod you lot. I'm gonna have a coffee.

[*Raghead goes over to the coffee machine. He pulls out an enormous amount of change*]

Raghead: Anyone want one?

Fat Jeff: [*Accusing voice*] You've been at that bleedin' tampax machine again Raghead. I've warned you about that.

Raghead: Well that's where you're wrong see, I won this lot on the bandit last night at the club. And besides that machine's empty this time of the month.

Fat Jeff: In that case I'll have fifteen with sugar.

Raghead: You can bugger off and get your own. You've just called me a thief.

Fat Jeff: But you are a thief.

[*Raghead gets his coffee and sits down*]

Raghead: [*To Fat Jeff*] But we're all thieves Jeff. I mean all there is to do all night at this dump is to wander around for stuff to pinch. In fact don't feel as though I've done a proper night's work unless my car boot is full.

Fat Jeff: [*Moral tone*] Well I don't need to pinch things. And I don't see why you should either. I mean it's me that takes the can.

Mary: Here, here Jeff, I totally agree with you.

Raghead: [*Big clever smile*] No Jeff, you don't take the can. [*Pause*] You take the cement mixers.

Fat Jeff: [*Suddenly all sheepish*] What cement mixer? I don't know what you're talking about.

Raghead: The big red one on wheels. I mean Jeff; you were about as subtle as a sledgehammer. We knew something big was going walkies when you turned up for a shift in a transit van saying you were in [*He starts to laugh*] 'the wife's wheels tonight'. So ya wife drives a ten ton builder's van eh Jeff?

Mary: [*Accusing voice*] So it was you who took the cement mixer then!!

Raghead: Me and Gus there, we were watching you at three o'clock in the morning from the factory window giving yourself a hernia. All you had to do was ask, and we'd have given you a hand.

Mary: [*Outraged*] We all got the blame for that.

Fat Jeff: [*All abashed*] Yeah but I'm bringing it back when the extensions finished.

Raghead: Come off it, your extension was finished weeks ago. We heard about the big posh house warming party you had for all the office knobs upstairs.

Big Gus: [*Looking over his paper disapprovingly*] Yeah, kept that one a secret dint ya.

Raghead: He didn't want the likes of us there, spoiling his big play for the day manager's job. We'd have lowered the tone wiv our roll-ups and Guinness.

Fat Jeff: It was just a small gathering of friends, that's all.

Raghead: Well if it was friends of yours, it would have been small. I bet the M.D. was there though!

Fat Jeff: [*All defensive*] Well if you must know he did pop in.

Big Gus: I bet you had an arse-licking contest.

Fat Jeff: It wasn't like that. I just wanted to give something back.

Raghead: What, like a cement mixer!

Fat Jeff: I wish you'd stop going on about that Raghead!! I've told you, I'm bringing it back. I just haven't got round to it yet.

Raghead: You've got a funny way of bringing it back by advertising it in the local paper for two hundred quid.

Fat Jeff: Two hundred and fifty actually, but I couldn't flog it so I will be bringing it back. Now will ya' shut up about that bleedin' cement mixer!!

Raghead: I'm not having a go Jeff. I'm just saying you're no different to us that's all. You just pretend you are 'cause you're the shift manager. But all that really means is that you get to pinch the big stuff.

Mary: Well to me a thief's a thief. It boils down to the way your parents bring you up. My parents made sure I never wanted for nothing. And look at me, I turned out all right.

[Everybody suddenly looks at Mary]

Fat Jeff: Well some of you were lucky to have two parents. I never knew my father.

Raghead: What, mother a bit loose was she?

Fat Jeff: [*Indignant*] No she bleedin' wasn't. The old sod pissed off when I was five. Never seen him since.

Mary: What, did he never send you a birthday card?

Fat Jeff: Funnily enough it was my fifth birthday when he slung his hook…I remember that day like it was yesterday. Left me and mum right up the creek he did. He was an alky see. All that year mum had been saving up a little money on the side just so I could have a bike for my birthday. [*Fat Jeff's expression goes all dreamy*] By hell I was excited that day. Dad took me down to the cycle shop. Mum had given him the money to get the bike. I tell ya my little heart was pounding. Suddenly there it was my little red tricycle hanging from the ceiling.

[Smiles to himself]

Raghead: [*Interrupting*] What!!! Five years old and ya couldn't ride a two-wheeler?

Malcolm: I remember my first bike. Dad got it off the ragman. He swapped it for an old blowlamp.

Raghead: Was that a three-wheeler like Jeff's then?

Malcolm: Nah, I wasn't a puff. In fact it didn't have any wheels.

Raghead: You sound about as lucky as Jeff.

Malcolm: The ragman said he had some wheels at his yard. He was going to drop them round. But he broke both his legs and fractured his skull when he fell off a ladder painting a house.

Raghead: So ya never got your wheels then?

Mary: That's a tragic story Malcolm.

Malcolm: Yeah it was terrible. Dad was in hospital for six weeks.

Fat Jeff: But I thought you said the ragman fell off the ladder?

Malcolm: Yeah he did. Burned real badly they said too.

[*Everybody is looking at each other mystified*]

Raghead: [*Big smile of inspiration*] I think I've sussed this one out Malcolm. I bet the ragman falling off the ladder had somfink to do wiv ya Dad's blowlamp.

Malcolm: [*Obviously*] Well yeah of course it did. It blew up while he was trying to light it. Lit up the sky for two streets, just like a roman candle. Mind you it made a lovely job of taking the paint off. Pity it took the roof off as well really.

Fat Jeff: How come your dad was injured then? Was he helping this bloke then strip the house?

Malcolm: Nah. The ragman was a gypsy ya see, and when his brothers found out what happened they kicked ten bells of shit outa him.

Raghead: [*Big smile*] There you are Jeff. We always get there in the end. Just persevere and follow the logic, and it's dead easy to make sense of Malcolm.

Malcolm: So instead of the bike I got a horse.

Raghead: [*Quickly answering*] The ragman's horse!!

Malcolm:[*Surprised*] Yeah, how did you know?

Raghead: [*Smiling at Malcolm*] You see after so long, you can suss him out. The clues are in his story.

Malcolm: What you on about Raghead?

Raghead: Never mind. What did you call this fine animal then Malcolm?

Malcolm: [*Mystified*] A horse, what do ya fink.

Raghead: [*To himself*] Well I asked for that one didn't I. It's name stupid!!

Malcolm: [*Excited*] Well the Lone Ranger was on telly in them days.

Raghead: So you called it! [*He gets out of his chair and makes like riding a horse and starts to sing the music*] Hey ho, hi yo Silver. [*All the rest join in banging hands on the table to the rhythm*] Ta ta tum ta ta tum ta ta tum tum tum ta ta tum ta ta tum ta ta tum tu tum ta tum ta tum ta ta tum tum tum

Malcolm: [*Big smile and singing*] Blackie!!

Mary: Blackie? But the Lone Ranger's horse was called Silver because it was white.

Malcolm: [*Obviously*] Well yeah I know. And mine was called blackie because it was black.

Raghead: [*Shaking head*] He always does it dun't he. He always catches us out. [*Raghead sits back down*] So what happened after you got this little red bike then Jeff? I bet you were the envy of the street eh?

Fat Jeff: Well that's just it I didn't get it did I.

Raghead: But I thought you said you went wiv ya old man to get it.

Fat Jeff: That's when he pissed off wannit. Just a minute son he said. Going to the shops to get some cigs he said. Thirty years later and he still hasn't turned up.

Raghead: Probably still in the queue in Asda.

Fat Jeff: Disappeared with my bike money and everything. Broke mum's heart it did. I'll never forgive him for that.

Mary: Bet you wouldn't recognise him now.

Fat Jeff: No, I don't think I would. I remember he had this cnormous black mole on one of his buttocks. I saw it one night when he fell off the toilet pissed. But I swear if I ever bump into him. [*He smacks his fist into his hand*]

[*Later in the shift in the canteen — Fat Jeff, Raghead, Big Gus, Mary, Malcolm and Black Dave are still sitting around the table reading their papers. From the back of the canteen in walk Monkey Hanger and Harry. As usual they are black from head to foot. There is a tramp with them, he is filthy and bearded and is carrying a plastic bag.*

Raghead's stare follows them. He is trying not to laugh. Fat Jeff is still reading his paper oblivious, as are Mary and Black Dave. Malcolm looks on dumbstruck.]

Harry: [*To tramp*] You just sit yourself down there mate and get yourself warm while I put the kettle on.

[*The tramp takes a seat next to Fat Jeff and puts his bag on the table. He starts to go through the ashtray. Monkey Hanger and Harry pick up their bags and go into the small adjoining open plan kitchen to make their supper*]

Raghead: Here have one of these mate [*He offers him a cigarette*]

[*Fat Jeff still oblivious reading the paper starts to sniff*]

Fat Jeff: [*To Mary*] Pooh open that window Mary it stinks in here.

Mary: Pooh it does, doesn't it. [*He gets up and then sees the tramp sitting next to Fat Jeff. He stands there staring*]

Fat Jeff: Well open the bleedin' window. [*He follows Mary's stare,* and turns to face the tramp] Evening. [*Turns back to Mary*] Well open the…..[*The penny drops. He turns back to face the tramp. A smile frozen on his face*] Harry! Monkey Hanger!! Could I have a word with you both for a moment?

[*Fat Jeff gets out of his chair, still smiling at the tramp. He goes over to the other side of the canteen with Harry and Monkey Hanger*]

Monkey Hanger: [*All innocent*] What is it like Jeff?

Fat Jeff: [*Whispering*] It's a tramp!

Harry: [*To Monkey Hanger*] So it's not Tom Jones then.

Monkey Hanger: Oh you mean Joe. And if you don't mind he's a gentleman of the road.

Fat Jeff: But what's he doing in here?

Monkey Hanger: He's gonna have a cuppa tea and some of me hot muffins.

Fat Jeff: [*Flippantly*] Oh well that's alright then… it may have escaped your notice, but this factory is a hygienic area. That man smells like a walking cesspit.

Harry: Oh here we go with your petty-minded prejudices. It doesn't matter that the poor old sod was freezing to death outside does it.

Fat Jeff: [*Pleading*] But lads I could lose my job if they find out I've had a tramp in the canteen.

Monkey Hanger: Eye man, and ya cud lose ya job if they find out where the cement mixer went anal.

Fat Jeff: You rotten sods. You wouldn't do that to a mate? [*Pauses and looks at them*] You wouldn't would you?

Monkey Hangar: [*Reassuring voice*] Cause we wouldn't Jeff, after he's had his tea and muffins, and a few hours kipp in the board-room, he'll be on his way by seven o'clock.

Fat Jeff: [*Panicking*] No, No! Not the boardroom, it's just been painted and decorated. He'll stink the place out.

Harry: That's very generous of you Jeff. So it's your office then?

Fat Jeff: On second thoughts, let's make it the boardroom [*Little laugh*] It's only them pansy directors. I'm off in the control room. If you get caught with him I haven't seen anything. I know nothing, nothing.

[*Fat Jeff scurries out of the canteen through the sound proof door. We hear the sound of machinery as the door opens and closes*]

Monkey Hanger: [*To tramp*] Now then my old mate. How many sugars in ya tea?

Tramp: You ain't got anything stronger have you?

Monkey Hanger: What like?

Tramp: Whisky, brandy, can of beer, meths?

Harry: What about it Raghead, any meths in the lab?

Raghead: I'm afraid the drink's globe is clean out of meths mate.

Tramp: What sorta lab do ya call that then? Can't be much cop if it dunt have any meths.

Malcolm: We've got some paraffin. How about a drop of that then?

Tramp: [*Big smile*] Now you're talking a real drink son.

Monkey Hanger: Well you heard the man Malcolm. Get the man a double paraffin on the house.

Malcolm: Right. [*He leaves to go into the lab next door*]

Tramp: Whose are them biscuits?

Raghead: Go on Mary give him a biscuit.

Mary: [*Indignantly effeminate voice*] If he thinks he's getting his grubby paws on my nuts he's got another thing coming.

[*Mary picks up his biscuits and sandwich box*]

Mary: I'm going to register my protests about this to Jeff. [*He exits angrily through the door*]

Tramp: What's up wiv the shirt-lifter then?

Black Dave: Oh he's just prejudice.

Tramp: Then you take no notice son.

[*Black Dave is forced to think about it. Malcolm comes back carrying a big brown lab bottle*]

Malcolm: Here it is. [*He gives the bottle to Raghead*]

Raghead: Just check the bottle. We don't want to poison you do we? [*Raghead checks the label*] That's the one Vintage alah Esso Blue. Get the man a mug Malcolm. Have you got no manners.

[*Malcolm slides a mug across the table. Raghead starts to pour*]

Raghead: Say when.

[*The tramp waits until it reaches the top*]

Tramp: When!! Just leave the bottle will ya.

[*All of them watch in amazement as the tramp downs the paraffin in one long swig. He slams the empty mug to the table, gives a satisfied groan and then burps.*]

Tramp: That hit the spot. [*He puts the cigarette Raghead gave him earlier into his mouth*] Got a light son?

Raghead: [*Weary*] I'd leave it a few minutes mate you don't want to make yourself sick.

[*Later in the canteen.*]

[*The tramp is licking clean his plate from which he has just eaten.*]

Malcolm: You was certainly hungry mate.

[*Raghead starts to roll himself a smoke*]

Raghead: You always been a tramp then?

Tramp: Nah, I was married once. Had a kid. [*He takes a couple of* *tabs out of the ashtray, puts one behind his ear, the other in his mouth*] You gotta light son?

Raghead: [*Giving him a light*] What happened then?

Tramp: Got married too young didn't I. We were having a real good time till the sprog came along. Horrible thing it was. All it did was cry all-night and shit all over the place. Then she started getting really awkward. [*Outraged*] Wanted me to get a job.

Harry: [*Sarcastic*] What a cow eh.

Monkey Hanger: What was ya last job like?

Tramp: [*Thinking hard*] I was once a milk monitor at school. But packed it in. Bloody hard work luggin those crates about, I can tell ya.

Raghead: What did ya do for money when ya got married?

Tramp: [*Smiling*] Sent her out for work of course. Mad on me she was. Helped her out an all. I got her three jobs. Morning down the washhouse. Afternoons cleaning in the pub. And evenings laying out stiffs at the Co-op Funeral Parlour. We were sitting pretty. So what did she go and do eh. Got herself pregnant didn't she. After eight months she had to give up her evening job. After that every-thing was different. I stuck it for five years. Then one day in a drunken haze I just slung my hook. Been on the road ever since.

Monkey Hangar: And you've never seen your kid since?

Tramp: Not for thirty years. And I don't bleedin want to either. In fact it was its' fifth birthday when I buggered off. Mind you got my own back for all them sleepless nights. [*He starts to laugh*] Our lass gave me twenty quid to get it a birthday present. Last time I saw that kid, the bloody fing was squawking it's eyes out in the bike shop.

[*Raghead, Big Gus and Malcolm all look at each other in shock. The story sounds familiar*]

Malcolm: [*All excited is frantically miming to everyone*] It's him, it's him!!

Harry: What's this Malcolm. Give us a clue?

Malcolm: [*Still miming*] It's him, it's him!!

[*Raghead winking and jerking his head artfully in a secret signal, gets out of his chair all bent and awkward*]

Harry: [*To Raghead*] Book or Film? The Hunchback of Notre Dame!!

Raghead: [*To tramp*] You don't mind if I have a quiet word with my mate do you. [*Raghead is still trying to secretly signal by winking and nodding*]

[*Harry and Monkey Hanger go with Malcolm, Big Gus and Raghead to the back of the canteen. They go into a huddle.*]

Malcolm: [*Fierce whisper*] It's him, It's him!!

Monkey Hanger: Who?

Malcolm: [*Whispering*] The dosser is Fat Jeff's dad.

Harry: Don't be stupid.

Malcolm: The only way to prove it is to look at his arse.

Raghead: Yeah, we've got to get a butchers of his arse.

[*Harry and Monkey Hanger stare warily at each other*]

Monkey Hanger: I sometimes have my doubts about you.

Raghead: No Malcolm's right. Fat Jeff said his old man was an alky; he disappeared when he was five. It was at the bike shop. He hasn't seen him since. He also said the only thing he could remember about him was he had a great big mole on his arse.

Harry: We'd better get to the bottom of this.

Raghead: So the only way to prove it is to get his kegs off.

Monkey Hanger: Well I think Mary is our resident expert in that department.

Raghead: Look we've got to be casual about this. Let's try the subtle approach. We just go casually back to the table and play it by ear. Use a bit of psychology.

They start super casually back to the table and sit back down. They are all smiling like a pack of hyenas. Malcolm is sitting directly opposite the tramp. Looking artfully at each other, all are waiting for the other to speak first. Malcolm takes it upon himself to have the first 'diplomatic' stab.

Malcolm: [*Winks to the others then turns to the tramp*] Eh mate………..show us your arse!!

Tramp: What's his game then. Is he a brown hatter or summat??

Monkey Hanger: Well thank you Sigmund Freud!

Tramp: [*To all of them*] So, that's why ya got me up here all friendly like. You're a load of arse bandits. It's a gangbang.

Monkey Hanger: No, you've got it all wrong mate.

Tramp: Well it'll cost ya. A quid for a look. Anything else is extra. And I'm warning ya now; I don't do any of that kinky stuff.

Monkey Hanger: Am I bloody hearing this or what?

Raghead: [*Getting up to explain*] No! It's nothing like that.

Tramp: [*Getting up slowly*] Now you just keep away from me. Don't try any rough stuff now. [*He puts his hand into his overcoat pocket, trying to pretend he has a gun*] I've got a gun in here. If ya come any closer I'll blow ya three piece sweet off.

[*He begins to back away as the lads slowly close on him. The tramps hand comes through a hole in the overcoat to expose his fingers pointing at them. Grabbing his carrier bag from the table he makes a bolt for the door*]

Raghead: Grab him lads!!

[*They all make a rush to grab him. Harry grabs him around the waist. Raghead gets his legs. Big Gus has his head. Monkey Hanger is caught in the middle of the tangle of bodies, with*

Malcolm holding him.]

Raghead: [*Shouting*] Somebody get his kegs down!!

[*In the confusion Malcolm is undoing Monkey Hanger's trousers. Harry has nearly got the tramps trousers off. The tramp manages to struggle onto all fours with his trousers around his knees showing his dirty underpants. Malcolm accidentally pulls down Monkey Hanger's trousers to around his ankles. A struggling Monkey Hanger gets to his feet only to fall straight onto the tramp's backside.*

At that moment Fat Jeff and Mary enter the canteen through the sound proof door. Everybody on the floor freezes and looks up at Fat Jeff and Mary. Monkey Hanger is in a very compromising position, with the tramp still on all fours, his trousers round his ankles and him on top, with his trousers round his knees.]

Fat Jeff: [*Shock*] Eye, eye!! What the bloody hell is going on in here then?

Monkey Hanger: [*All embarrassed*] Hello Jeff. Come and meet your Dad!!

[*Fat Jeff recognises his dad and starts chasing him round the canteen kicking the tramp/his dad up the backside.*]

38

THE SWORD OF REDUNDANCY

Tony Hall

It is the start of the shift. Everyone, except Raghead, is looking at the notice board, gossiping and looking very worried.

A Notice reads:

DUE TO THE NEED FOR COST CUTTING THE COMPANY WILL BE BRINGING IN AN EMPLOYMENT CONSULTANT WITH THE VIEW TO CUTTING STAFF COSTS. THIS MAY INCLUDE THE NEED FOR COMPULSORY REDUNDANCIES WE HOPE ALL STAFF WILL CO-OPERATE IN THIS EXERCISE.

Monkey Hanger: That's a bit rich innit man.' hope the staff will co-operate' That's like asking a condemned man to help the executioner.

Big Gus: [*Panicking*] Bloody 'ell I've just promised our lass to get the house re-wired.

Malcolm: This'll be a shock then.

Mary: Never mind your re-wiring. Courtney and I have just had a new bathroom fitted complete with new bidet and toilet suite.

Malcolm: Sounds like that's down the pan.

Mary: But we're up to our eyes in plastic money.

Harry: That's all I need redundancy. I've just booked a holiday to Disneyland.

Malcolm: Who needs Disneyland when you've got this Mickey Mouse outfit.

Black Dave: Oh shit, I've just ordered double-glazing.

Malcolm: That's well out the window now.

Big Gus: I was gonna get me haemorrhoids done private.

Malcolm: That's a real pain in the arse innit. What about you Jeff?

[Everyone is now fed up of Malcolm having a pun for every answer.)

Fat Jeff: Actually I was taking our lass on a second honeymoon to the Great Barrier Reef in Australia after we had been trekking on mules in the Himalayas for two weeks.

[Everyone is staring at Malcolm. There is a long pause and no forthcoming pun.]

Malcolm: Oh right. She'll be disappointed then. You'll have to use the carrot and stick if you want to go down under on her then.

[At that moment Raghead comes through into the canteen]

Monkey Hanger: Eh Raghead have you seen this?

Raghead: Sodding hell ain't ya got the kettle on!

Fat Jeff: That's Raghead, always gets his priorities right.
[Raghead puts the kettle on and takes his seat and starts to read one of a pile of papers]

Monkey Hanger: Bugger the kettle Raghead!! What about this?

[*He points to the notice*]

Raghead: [*Not bothered*] Oh yeah I've read it.

Harry: Well ain't ya worried?

Raghead: Well I'm alright, it dunt effect me. They'll probably just be clearing out the chaff.

Fat Jeff: Well that puts you at the top of the list Raghead.

Raghead: Look who's talking? That's the first time I've seen you without a canteen chair stuck to ya arse.

Fat Jeff: I'm management mate. Me and the MD are like that.

[*Fat Jeff crosses his fingers and smirks. Raghead smugly shakes his head*]

Raghead: All the brown nosing you've done over these years in't worth a fart mate. When the big boys upstairs put pen to paper, you're nothing more than a figure in the fixed costs balance sheet. And you're a bigger figure than all of us mate. You stick out like a sore thumb on the balance sheet.

Monkey Hanger: Yeah, if they get rid of you the MD can move up to a seven series BMW next year. I bet they won't be getting rid of all those company cars.

Big Gus: Always the bloody same innit. We get a kick up the arse for our loyalty, and management get a new car. I'm gonna see the union about this.

Monkey Hanger: Well don't bleedin bother last time that union rep got involved, we ended up on less money, less holidays and he ended up driving a bigger car than the lot of them.

Raghead: About as useful as a one legged man at an arse kicking competition that union.

[*They all move over to the table and sit down with Raghead*]

Fat Jeff: So what makes you think you're so fire proof then

Raghead. The last time you did any work was nicking that lead off the storeroom.

Raghead: Use ya brains mate. I'm like a protected species I am.

Malcolm: Like an elephant ya mean?

Fat Jeff: Moves about the same speed.

Monkey Hanger: You mean the old colour card Raghead?

Raghead: Exactly

Black Dave: That's you and me both then.

Raghead: Sorry mate. There's only room in this lifeboat for one and that's moi.

Black Dave: You can't stop me mate.

Fat Jeff: *(Laughing)* That's right. He's got on better odds than you.

Raghead: You reckon do ya?

Fat Jeff: He's black you're brown.

Monkey Hanger: Now that's why Jeff is management. Dunt miss nowt.

Big Gus: As razor sharp as a house brick.

Raghead: But it dunt work like that. Ya know the saying. If ya white, that's alright, if ya brown stick around, if ya black get back. Dave would have a better chance if he were white.

Harry: So that's you're card marked Dave. So ya reckon the rest of us will be alright Raghead?

Raghead: Well what ya gotta think is, is I'm in the middle sort of. To management ways of thinking I represent both the black and white card. Keep me and ya can get rid of any of you lot and nobody can complain discrimination. I tell ya I could've been a Channel Four newsreader.

Malcolm: You're name's not Chakarabarte.

Mary: Well what about me? I'm a minority group.

Raghead: Oh yeah, you'll be alright as well. Shirtlifters are protected as well these days.

Mary: The only thing is... How will this consultant person know.....I'm Ya know?

> [*The crew all look at each other, and then at Mary.*]

Big Gus: [*Obviously*] Oh you'll be alright in that department Mary.

Mary: [*To Raghead*] You and I should stick together Raghead now that we've got something in common. [*He winks at Raghead*]

Harry: What about us normal blokes?

Raghead: No such thing as normal these days mate. We live in politically correct world. You lot are the odd ones out.

Fat Jeff: Bloody marvelous. So you've either got to be a queer or black to keep ya job.

Raghead: That's unless you're Ukrainian.

Fat Jeff: Ukrainian!! What the bleedin' 'ell have they got to do with it?

Raghead: You should read the Guardian mate. They're another protected species like me and Mary.

Big Gus: So to keep ya job, you have to be black, queer or Ukrainian.

Raghead: Or Jewish.

Malcolm: That's an idea. I'll become Jewish.

> [*Raghead pulls out a rusty knife*]

Raghead: Shall I do the honours then Malc?

> [*Malcolm cringes*]

Malcolm: What about Ukrainian?

Harry: That's not fair

Raghead: Ya know the only person who uses a word like "fair" is the working man. That's a word that's not in the management dictionary. Take my cousin for instance, do you know when he came to this country, wounded and everything after fighting for his country in the Gulf war. He only got a pension after taking the government to court. That's fairness for ya.

Mary: Typical that is. We don't even treat our fighting men properly.

Big Gus: That's terrible. What unit was he in?

Raghead: The Republican Guard.

Fat Jeff: Ya know Raghead you talk a load of bollocks.

Raghead: Well you'll be first out the door. Middle management these days, not a safe job my old son. You have to get yourself an edge, and you haven't got one. Then you had loads of time on sick last year, that's gonna be a big black mark against your name.

Fat Jeff: They can't count that. That was executive stress the doctor said. That's why he gave me ten weeks on sick.

Big Gus: Is that how long it took ya to finish your extension?

Raghead: Yeah that's right, another week and you'd have got the roof finished.

Fat Jeff: Now talk like that can cost a man his job.

Mary: Then there's the cement mixer. That's another black mark against you Jeff.

Harry: That's right, management have got their suspicions about who took that. And we all know where to look.

[The lads all stare at Fat Jeff. Fat Jeff gets up all indignant.]

Fat Jeff: What ya looking at me like that for. I'm not sitting here taking this off you lot. We'll see who gets the boot first. And if I have any say in it, you'll be signing on first Raghead.

44

Raghead: In your dreams.

[*Fat Jeff goes to the factory door adjoining the canteen.*]

Fat Jeff: And you lot can get ya arses outa of here, this factory dunt run itself [*He glares at them*] Cement mixer eh? Well I know who my mates are now.

[*Some time later Raghead is in the canteen alone. He is drinking tea, smoking and reading the paper. Black Dave enters the canteen all artful and sits down near Raghead*]

Black Dave: This redundancy stuff is really worrying me Raghead.

Raghead: So it should mate.

Black Dave: What you woz saying before like about all this colour business. Do ya really think it works?

Raghead: Well course it does. Everybody's got to work to colour quotas these days.

Black Dave: Yeah but how does that work for me like?

Raghead: Look mate, I told ya. You'd have a better chance if ya were white. In fact, not just white but like really white. You would stand a better chance than that lot. But ya can't do anything about ya colour can ya. [*Black Dave has a curious expression on his face*]

[*Later Raghead is back in the canteen by himself, still smoking, drinking tea and reading newspapers. From the back of the canteen, Malcolm, Harry, Mary and Big Gus enter and sit down to join Raghead. The three of them are looking at each other artfully whilst Raghead reads the paper. They start to pour the tea.*]

Big Gus: You seem to be well up on all this racial stuff Raghead. Do you really think it makes all that difference?

Raghead: Well look at me. You lot are all a bag of nerves, and do I look worried? [*Mary, Harry, Malcolm and Big Gus all look at each other.*]

[*Later Raghead is still in the canteen smoking, drinking and reading. This time it is Fat Jeff that comes to join him. He too is all artful. Raghead looks up. Fat Jeff gives him a big patronizing smile and goes into his pocket for money and goes over to the coffee machine.*]

Fat Jeff: Cup of coffee Raghead?

[*Raghead is all surprised and puts down his mug*]

Raghead: Don't mind if I do. This ones a dead soldier. I'll have a seventeen with sugar.

[*Fat Jeff comes over with coffees and gives Raghead his. He then gets out his sandwich box and takes out a sandwich. He offers Raghead one. Raghead looks suspicious*]

Fat Jeff: Roast beef off the bone.

[*Gratefully Raghead takes the sandwich*]

Raghead: Cheers Jeff, your lass looks after you.

[*Jeff suddenly breaks down with crocodile tears.*]

Fat Jeff: Well she won't if I get made redundant. Ya gotta help me Raghead. Our lass is too used to the good life to get use to queuing up to cash my unemployment giro. Please Raghead you've gotta help me.

Raghead: Alright, alright.

Fat Jeff: What am I gonaa do Raghead?

Raghead: Well there might be a long shot. [*Raghead is thinking, He suddenly shakes his head*] Nah ya wouldn't do it.

Fat Jeff: I will!! I will!! I'll try anything.

Raghead: Alright.

[*Later in the shift everybody is in the canteen drinking, smoking and reading. Malcolm seems to have something on his mind.*]

Malcolm: [*To everybody*] What's a bidet? [*The shift all look at each other*]

Raghead: Well that came from nowhere dint it?

[*At that precise moment the company secretary enters the canteen and pins another notice on the board. She is a typical blond bimbo type and gorgeous*]

Big Gus: Bloody 'ell you're working ' late.

Secretary: Got a lot to do because of all these cut backs. I've been using the MD's Dictaphone.

Raghead: Can't ya use you're finger like everybody else.

Secretary: You lot 'ave all got to be here early tomorrow. Ya all gonna be interviewed by this consultant bloke. Oh especially you Raghead, and Mary. You two are in first.

Raghead: [*Big smile*] Told ya.

Fat Jeff: Just a minute. What about the rest of us? How come they're get special treatment?

Secretary: Well I don't know do I.

Fat Jeff: Why can't I go in early? [*All flustered the secretary looks at her clipboard*]

Secretary: Well I'm sorry but you can't. Oh just a minute. You're not Ukrainian are you?

Fat Jeff: No I bloody am not.

Secretary: Pity. Sorry then. [*She exits*]

[*The whole shift gets up, except Raghead and goes to the notice. Fat Jeff suddenly starts laughing and looking in Raghead's directions. Then the rest of the crew read it and look in Raghead's direction.*]

Raghead: What's tickling you lot?

Fat Jeff: [*Cleverly laughing*] Look at this Raghead. As far as you're concerned, your theory goes out the window. Look who they've brought in.[*Fat Jeff reads aloud the name of the name of* *the consultant doing the interviews*] Mr Ariel Sharonski Rosenburg. A good old Yorkshire name if I ever heard one. He'll have you Raghead!! [*Raghead's face is frozen in shock*]

[*The next night the secretary is seen entering the canteen with smart dressed gentlemen wearing a Jewish scull cap. He is obviously the outside employment consultant. He is carrying a clipboard*]

Secretary: Well I told them to be early so they should all be in…..

[*She stops dead in her tracks as she enters the canteen. She is in shock. Malcolm is dressed like a Cossack complete with fur hat. Harry is blacked up with a tight black curly wig.*

Next to Harry, Black Dave is wearing a blond wig with a pasty white face. Mary is dressed to ensure there is no doubt he is Gay, complete with beret and made up face. Monkey Hanger has dreadlocks and a big woollen Rasta hat on.

Big Gus is dressed in full Scottish attire with kilt and holding bagpipes. Jeff is conspicuous for his absence, as is Raghead]

Secretary*: [Sort of trying to keep her composure*] Well who do you want to start with? Raghead was supposed to be first, but he's not here.

Harry: [*Quietly*] Raghead's bottled it.

Big Gus: So's Jeff.

Consultant: I'll start with the shift supervisor.

Secretary: He doesn't seem to be here yet either.
[*Suddenly we hear a voice in the background with a very bad Asian accent*]

Fat Jeff: [*Asian accent*] My most gracious appologies Sahib for my lateness. [*Fat Jeff is browned up and wearing a Sikh turban.*) I have been at the Temple for Hari Krishna. [*The consultant and Fat*

Jeff enter the consultant's office. The consultant sits behind his desk and opens a file in front of him and puts on his glasses]

Consultant: [*Reading file*]   Mmmmm....What does the G stand for in your middle name?

Fat Jeff: Gupta, Sahib.

Consultant: You seem to have had a lot of time sick last year? [*Fat Jeff is seen swallowing hard*] It has also been brought to my attention about the large amount of company property that goes missing on your shift......For instance a cement mixer. [*Jeff is by now terrified*]

[*Jeff is seen backing into the canteen from the Consultant's office. He is seen bowing.*]

Fat Jeff: Thank you, thank you Sahib. And may the Great One shine his torch onto your house. A thousand blessings be upon you.

[*With the groveling over Jeff turns to the rest of the shift who are sat in a line waiting.*]

Harry: Bloody 'ell your putting it on a bit thick.

Fat Jeff: He's a right bleedin' animal.

Harry: Who's next?

Fat Jeff: Taras Bulba there. Just a minute you remind me of somebody Harry......Have you ever been in The Four Tops?

Harry: At least I don't look like Gunga Din. Eh guess what Raghead hasn't turned up.

Fat Jeff: Well that's one good thing to come out of it. This bloke is gonna squeeze him till his pips squeak.

[*Back in the consultant's office he is looking at a personnel file. He then looks over his glasses at Malcolm on the other side of his desk and smiles.*]

Consultant: So you're Ukrainian? I don't think we need to go any further. [*The consultant closes his file*]

　　[*Malcolm is seen re-entering the canteen after his interview.*]

Monkey Hanger: Well how did it go?

Malcolm: Eh, Raghead was right.

Fat Jeff: Did he say anything about me?

Malcolm: I've been sworn to secrecy. But I will say this. I've enjoyed working with you and I'll be sad to see you leave. I'm sorry I can't tell you anything else.

Fat Jeff: Bloody lumbago!! I knew it wouldn't work. I'm gonna kill Raghead when I get me hands on.

Malcolm: Where is he?

Monkey Hanger: I think he knows the game's up.

Malcolm: Well that's handy for you then Jeff?

Fat Jeff: What is?

Malcolm: Raghead lives just near you. He can pick you up when you both go to sign on. You'll save loads on petrol 'cause you don't get much on the dole, and at your age I think you might have some trouble finding a job.

Fat Jeff: Bloody hell, why don't you just give me the rope!

Mary: Mind you there's always B & Q. They prefer the more mature person. You'll cut quite a fetching figure in that little red apron.

Fat Jeff: I wish you lot would shut up!! I haven't gone yet. And who knows, a few of you might be following me.

　　[*At that precise moment a loud voice shouts angrily into the canteen.*]

Consultant: Next!!

　　[*Back in the consultant's office he is again looking at a file. He looks over his glasses at Big Gus dressed in his full Scottish costume with ginger wig and bagpipes.*]

Consultant: You know I've always loved the Scottish pipes. [*Big Gus swallows hard*]

[*Back in the canteen the entire shift are sitting nervously waiting. Suddenly the sound of a cat being strangled enters the canteen. Only it is Big Gus trying to play the bagpipe. We suddenly hear the consultant's voice angrily entering the canteen.*]

Consultant: OUT!!!

[*The shift all look at each other with shocked faces. Big Gus comes slowly into the canteen looking deflated.*]

Fat Jeff: Never mind Gus. You can have a lift as well.

[*Suddenly Big Gus starts dancing a high land fling.*]

Big Gus: No need!! Raghead's a genius!! You're next Harry.

Fat Jeff: Well it didn't bloody work for me.

[*A few minutes later Harry's blacked up face is seen coming back into the canteen and Harry is seen punching the air in delight.*]

Harry: Yesssss!!

[*The entire shift is dancing around except Fat Jeff who is nearly in tears.*]

Fat Jeff: That's right, you lot look after yourselves. Don't think about me sleeping on the streets will ya.

[*The consultant comes into the canteen and goes over to Fat Jeff.*]

Consultant: Why such a long face? You should be happy like your friends.

Fat Jeff: They've got something to be happy about. They've still got a job.

Consultant: And so have you. [*Fat Jeff's face suddenly lights up and he jumps up and kisses the consultant. He joins in the* *dancing with the shift*] There's only this Raghead fellow to interview now. Does anyone know where he is?

[*The shift suddenly stop celebrating and all look at each other with concerned faces.*]

Consultant: I can tell you I'm not impressed.

[*Suddenly a figure is in the canteen doorway. It is Raghead and he is dressed all in black complete with false beard in the guise of an orthodox Jew.*]

Raghead: Shalom!!

[*He moves towards the consultant in a traditional Hebrew dance and shoulder to shoulder they start dancing. The shift all join in.*]

HOSTAGES TO A FORTUNE

The scene is of a typical factory canteen. The episode opens with a group shot of all the shift except Fat Jeff gathered around the canteen table. As usual the table is a right mess with tea mugs, newspapers etc, all over the place. The shift is gathered around a radio on the canteen table, but it is not a radio, it is a scanner and they are listening in to the local police frequency. The lads are listening intensely to the scanner. A very sexy sounding police-woman is on the radio.

Female Police voice: This is Alpha Bravo to control — we are in pursuit of joyriders travelling at speed in easterly direction — over?

Monkey Hanger: Cooo what a voice, she sounds sexy, aintt coppers in uniform annall.

Big Gus: She might be a right dog. Ya can't tell from a voice.

Monkey Hanger: With a voice like that, she can try my helmet for size anytime.

Police Control voice: This is control Alpha Bravo, we have an urgent request, do you copy over?

Female Police Voice: Alpha Bravo receiving over?

Police Control: Are you in vicinity of Abdul's fish and chip shop over?

Raghead: Eh that's my cousin's shop!! What's going on there then? [*They all start to listen intently*]

Mary: I know that place. I had jumbo sausage there once. I was ill for days. Sickness and diarrhea chronic I had. My backside was like a blood orange.

Big Gus: Never heard of that, a jumbo sausage giving you a sore arse.

Malcolm: Are you sure it was the jumbo sausage that did it?

Mary: [*All indignant.*] I don't know what you mean!!

Malcolm: Well it could've been something else you ate.

Mary: Well Courtney did think it might have been the stuffing.

Raghead: Ya wanna try eating it next time then.

[At that precise moment Fat Jeff comes through from the door adjoining the factory to the canteen. We hear the noise of the factory as the door opens.]

Fat Jeff: Well this is a bloody surprise. It's like the Mary Celeste in that factory.

Big Gus: It's tea break in half an hour.

Fat Jeff: Never mind that. Get that pump fixed.

Big Gus: Why ya picking on me?

Fat Jeff: Cause you're the shift engineer.

Big Gus: Oh yeah.

Fat Jeff: Well come on then!!

Big Gus: I'm just finishing me tea.

Fat Jeff: [*Raging*]: The factory's ground to a halt. *I 've got a* two million pound high tech computerised digital state of the art thermal cooling pump needs fixing. And he wants to finish his tea!!

Big Gus: [*Stands up*]: Alright, alright. Ya like an old woman. Where's me hammer?

[All the lads are still listening to the Police on the scanner.]

Police Controller voice: We have an armed robbery in progress at the fish shop.

Raghead: Armed robbery? He's got nowt worth nicking.

Fat Jeff: What ya listening to?

Harry: Radio four, The Archers.

[Fat Jeff sits down to listen and starts to pour himself a mug of tea]

Fat Jeff: Turn it up I missed yesterday's episode.

[Malcolm turns it up.]

Female Police voice: Alpha Bravo ten four breaking off hot pursuit.

Police Controller Voice: Approach area with caution reports of shots fired, armed unit responding, helicopter overhead reports fish shop on fire.

[All the lads are listening intensly]

Fat Jeff: Bloody hell, this is exciting! It's getting more like East Enders every episode.

Female Police Voice: Alpha Bravo to control — suspects have left the scene and am in pursuit south towards the docks. Two suspects, one black and one white driving a pink Lada.

Monkey Hanger: Wunt be seen dead in a Lada.

Mary: That means they're heading in this direction.

[All the lads go to the canteen window except Jeff who has his ear pressed to the scanner still believing he is listening to the Archers]

Female Police Voice: Alpha Bravo to control, we're losing them.

Fat Jeff:[*Into radio*] Go on, get ya foot down.

[We hear the sound of Police Sirens.]

Harry: Look, there they are!

Raghead: Eh, they're coming past the window.

[Police sirens getting louder]

Fat Jeff: [*Into radio*] Bloody hell these sound effects are good.

[We hear screeching tyres]

Monkey Hanger: Where they gone?

Harry: Round the back. See that cop car move!

Female Police voice: Alpha Bravo to control. Suspects have abandoned car and entered a nearby factory. Please advise?

Fat Jeff: [*Into radio*] Call for back-up ya silly sod!

[*Suddenly the shift are stiff with fear and looking at the two wide eyed youths looking at them with sawn off shotguns. The white youth is also carrying a holdall. Jeff is still listening to the "radio"*]

Fat Jeff: Eh Raghead get the kettle on this tea's cold.

White Youth: Right everybody get their hands up!!

Fat Jeff:[*Into radio*] Bloody hell they must have got new script writers. Ambridge 'll never be the same again.

[*The black youth has come over to the table and has the shotgun at the back of Jeff's head*]

Black Youth: Eh Fatso get ya hands up!!

[*Fat Jeff has noticed that the lads all have their hands up*]

Fat Jeff: It's only a play ya know.

[*He suddenly turns round and is looking down the barrel of the shotgun. He looks at the youth and then at the radio.*]

Black Youth: Over there and hands up, or I'll blow your bald ugly head off.

Fat Jeff: Do you mind.. I just listening..... Bloody hells bells and umbreago!! Where did you come from?

Black Youth: Get over there baldy and shut up!!

[*Fat Jeff gets to his feet and puts his hands up*]

Fat Jeff: Do you know you're trespassing? Raghead, call the Police. [*We hear the sound of lots of Police cars pulling up with sirens blazing.*]

Fat Jeff: That was bloody quick.

White Youth: Right away from the window!! Sit down!! And keep your hands where we can see 'em. Try owt and fatso gets both barrels.

Monkey Hanger: I got an idea. Let's rush 'em, Raghead.

Raghead: Mine's better.

Monkey Hanger: What's that?

Raghead: You rush 'em.

[*Police scanner starts up again*]

Female Police Voice: Alpha Bravo to control. We have the building surrounded. We may have a possible hostage situation.

Black Youth: Eh they've got a scanner. That's handy. Don't you lot know ya breaking the law listening to one of them. [*Suddenly from outside a Police loudhailer.*]

Police Loudhailer: [*Voice only*] The place is surrounded. Just put the guns down and come out quietly.

White Youth:[*To Raghead*] You! Come here!!

Raghead: Who me?

White Youth: Come here!! [*He goes over to Raghead and grabs him round the neck and puts the shot gun to his head.*]

Fat Jeff: Eh just take it easy son. Now you don't want to hurt anybody. [*Jeff moves closer and stretches out his hand.*] Why don't you just give me the gun.

White Youth: Take another step and I'll blow his head off. [*Jeff pretends to be all calm just like in the movies*]

Fat Jeff: Now you don't mean it. Just give me the gun. Don't worry Raghead I don't think he'll do it.

Raghead: Can't you be a bit more positive?

White Youth: I'm telling ya, I'll pull the trigger!! Now stay back Fatso.

Fat Jeff: Go on then pull the trigger. You ain't got the Bottle.

Raghead: Well if ya do point it in his direction.

Fat Jeff: He's bluffing. [*Suddenly the white youth points his gun and tries to fire but it does not go off.*]

White Youth: What's up wiv this thing?

Malcolm: Ya not gonna get far wiv the safety catch on.

White Youth: Oh yeah, cheers mate.

[*He takes off the safety catch, and the gun goes off blasting the microwave to bits*]

Fat Jeff: That's company property that is.

Harry: Bloody hell my lasagne was in there.

Black Youth: He means it mate.

[*Raghead is still choking in the head lock.*]

Raghead: Well don't mind me will ya. I can't breath.

[*The white youth pushes Raghead aside and grabs Fat Jeff round the neck and this time puts the gun to his head. He starts to drag Jeff to the window.*]

White Youth: There's one more barrel left for you fatso.

Raghead: Just a minute.

White Youth: What?

[*Raghead is determined to get his own back on Jeff*]

Raghead: Just put down the gun.

White Youth: Come any closer and and he gets it.

Fat Jeff: Raghead!! Raghead! Just stay back. He means it.

Raghead: Don't worry Jeff he's only bluffing. Ya said so yourself.

Police Loudhailer: This is the Police. What's happening in there?

[*The white youth drags Jeff to the window and opens it. He shouts at the Police outside.*]

White Youth: I'm warning ya. Back off. We've got hostages in here.

[*A voice over the Police scanner.*]

Male Police Voice: Alpha Bravo to control. A suspect has just brought a hostage to the window.

Harry: Where's the bird copper gone?

Police Voice Controller: Can you give a description, over?

Male Police Voice: Some fat bald bloke.

[*Fat Jeff hearing the words over the scanner is suddenly indignant. He shouts back at the Police*]

Fat Jeff: Who are you calling fat and bald!!?.. four eyes. Call ya self Police. Ya couldn't Police a chimps' tea party.

Police Voice Controller: We have a trained negotiator on the way.

Another Police Voice: It's SWAT control here. What's MO on this one? Negotiator keeps them talking and we go in?

Police Voice Controller: Looks like it. Just as long as you don't make a mess like last time. Bodies all over the place.

SWAT Officer: Don't worry, they won't know what hit them. I've got my glasses on this time.

White Youth: So that's the game is it? [*To black friend.*] *You cover* that door. [*He lets Jeff go.*] Sit down and don't move!

[*The lads round the table are whispering*]

Harry: Bloody hell, what did he mean by that "right mess last time"?

Mary: Bodies all over the place.

Malcolm: What we gonna do?

Fat Jeff: Just remember we shouldn't panic. I've got a plan, it's gonna take precise timing, skill, courage, cunning, brains, tenacity, bottle, [*The lads round the table start yawning*]...... nerve, flair, invention, daring, guts, defiance, audacity......

Raghead: Wake me up when he's finished.

Harry: Alright, alright!! What is it!!?

[*With that statement Fat Jeff suddenly runs to the window opens it and jumps out shouting.*]

Fat Jeff: *GERONIMO!!!*

[*The lads sit there looking at each other in disbelief. They hear a scream and a crash and they all rush to the window, including the criminals.*]

Black Criminal: [*Laughing*] Ha, ha, ha he landed right on top of that cop van. Who's he think he is, Bat Man?

Big Gus: Eh look there's TV cameras and it looks like local radio down there.

Black Dave: Look there it's the MD talking to the Radio people.

Raghead: Switch the radio on.

[*The lads switch a radio on and tune in to the local station. The factory MD is on the air*]

Radio Reporter: Several of your staff are still being held hostage at gun point. And one has just been thrown out the window by these vicious criminals, causing extensive damage to a nearby Police Van. Can you comment on that?

Black Criminal: What's that about!! Vicious criminals!!

MD: [*Voice only*] Well vehicles parked in that area, do so at their own risk, and we cannot be held responsible for damage. What I would like to add is that our products are still the best value for money, with fast delivery service that is second to none.

60

Raghead: Bloody typical. He's giving 'em a sales pitch.

Radio Reporter: From his stretcher we can speak with the hostage who has just been thrown from the window.

Black Youth: We never touched him!

Fat Jeff: [*Voice on radio*] I did all I could for the lads in there. Dragged one the thugs to the ground as he threatened the staff, and fought off the other with a gun still pointing to my head.

Radio reporter: And did the other staff help you?

Fat Jeff: [*Voice on Radio*] Understandably they froze, having been under fire in the forces when I was in the Gulf, I instinctively remembered my training.

Harry: Lying sod. He was in the Territorial Army stores.

Big Gus: Nearest he's been to the Gulf is Bognor Regis.

Radio Reporter: And as the emergency services take the hero of the moment to hospital.....

White Youth: [*To black youth*] We better talk about this. [*To rest*] We're just over there, so any of ya move and.. [*He shows them the shotgun*]

[*The two criminals retreat to the back of the canteen to talk. The radio reporter comes back onto the radio.*]

Radio Reporter: We can further report that the two desperate armed robbers who are at this moment holding several factory labourers hostage...

Mary: Factory labourers! Cheeky sod! [*All the crew shhhh him to listen*]

Radio Reporter: Earlier this evening they got away with over two hundred thousand pounds in cash after robbing Abdul's Fish Shop. The proprietor, Mr Abdul also stated he had also been savagely beaten to the ground and further robbed of his Rolex watch. Mr Abdul went on that they also took his full set of Tiger

Woods golf clubs, and his deep sea fishing tackle. We now return you to the studios for the controversial Walt Risdale soap box hour. And this week Walter has as his guest local councillor Bert Lumsden. Walt will be putting the councillor on the spot over where he stands on dog muck.

[*Raghead switches off the radio*]

Raghead: Did you hear that!! Now that's interesting.

Malcolm: Yeah, there's tons of dog shit near our house.

Black Dave: Our verge is covered.

Raghead: The two hundred grand. Idiot!!

Harry: I've bet they've got it in that holdall.

Big Gus: That's a lot of money.

Black Dave: Bloody is.

Malcolm: That's forty thousand each.

Raghead: I say we jump 'em when we get the chance.

[*The lads all look at each other. The white and the black criminal are looking out the window. The remains of the shift are sat round the table with the white criminal who still has the gun. Suddenly the radio scanner starts up again. It is the police.*]

SWAT officer: I have two suspects in sights. Can I open fire?

Harry: [*To Black Dave and black criminal*] Hey get down!!!

[*Black Dave and the criminal both look at each other, slap palms and start to dance.*]

Raghead: Now!!!

[*The shift suddenly jump on both the criminals and disarm them. Raghead is now covering them with one shotgun and Black Dave with the other shotgun*]

Raghead: Quick get some rope and tie them up. [*Raghead gives the gun to Big Gus*] Keep them covered, I'll go see the coppers, and keep away from the windows, that lot are trigger happy out there.

[*Raghead goes to the canteen door. The shift do not notice that he has artfully picked up the holdall, and is out the door. Big Gus is pointing the gun at them with a look of melodramatic pleasure*]

Big Gus: Go on, make my day.

[*It is some time later and Raghead still has not come back.*]

Monkey Hanger: Where the bleedin' 'ell is Raghead?

Harry: Yeah he's takin' his time.

[*Suddenly scanner starts up.*]

Police Officer Voice: Somebody has just run from the back carrying a holdall. Suspect is making a get-away in the Pink Lada.

Black Criminal: [*Hands tied*] Bloody cheek, somebody is nicking our car!!

[*Harry rushes through the canteen exit and then rushes back. He notices that the holdall has gone.*]

Harry: It's Raghead doing a runner!! And he's took the holdall.

Monkey Hanger: He's ripping us off!!

Mary: I knew he was up to something!!

Big Gus: He'll be on his way to the airport with the money, knowing him.

Malcolm: Yeah, Switzerland or somewhere.

White Criminal: [*Hand's tied*] What's your mate's nicked our car and took the holdall for?

Monkey Hanger: The money, what else.

Black Criminal: What money?

Big Gus: The two hundred grand in the holdall that you two nicked from the chip shop you burnt down.

[*The criminals start laughing to themselves.*]

Monkey Hanger: What ya laughing at?

Harry: It aint funny. He's supposed to be a mate!! We were gonna share it.

Malcolm: Yeah, forty grand each. And Raghead's took the lot *now.*

[*The two criminals cannot stop laughing*]

Black Dave: It aint that funny.

White Criminal: Oh yes it is. There aint no two hundred grand.

Monkey Hanger: That's what it said on the radio.

Black Criminal: We never robbed no chip shop. We were on our way to do the job when we stopped off for some grub.

White Criminal: Yeah that Abdul fella was setting it alight for an insurance job when we got there. We bolted when the shop blew up.

Harry: So what's in the holdall then?

White Criminal: [*To Black criminal*] Tell 'em.

Black Criminal: Jumbo sausage and chips twice!!!

[*The black and white criminals are in hysterics.*]

RAGHEAD'S PIE

In this episode only the lads are joined by the following characters:
Guardian photographer / reporter
Art Expert : Sir Jago Bagshot-Ponsenby Smythe.
Female Assistant: Lady Nigella, Arksworth-Fortescue.

[*The lads are sitting in the canteen smoking, drinking tea and engrossed in the newspapers. Malcolm is reading The Guardian, the rest reading various tabloids. Fat Jeff is engrossed in a drawing on a scrap of paper. Monkey Hanger is working something out on a calculator.*
Monkey Hanger shakes his head in despair at the figures on the calculator.]

Monkey Hanger: I tell ya man my arse is scraping on the floor this month. I'm flat broke.

Raghead: It's that lass of yours mate. She spends money like ya pull it out ya backside.

Fat Jeff: [*Looking up from drawing*] That's what I like about you Raghead, you always have an intellectual contribution to make to the conversation.

Raghead: Well look who's talking. Ya hardly a candidate for Question Time ya-self mate.

Big Gus: Raghead's got a point though. If my missus wanted to spend seven hundred pounds on a pair of curtains like Monkey Hanger's I'd put my foot-down. Ya gotta be firm wiv women. Show 'em who's the boss.

Monkey Hanger: Aye I did put me foot right down on that one. And ya know what she said. I'll not get me leg over until I changed me mind.

Big Gus: Bloody blackmail that!! I hope ya stuck to ya guns?

65

Monkey Hanger: Well course I did man. There was no way I was standing for that. A nooky strike.

Fat Jeff: [*Laughing*] What ya do. Pick it?

Monkey Hanger: No after intense negotiations later that night in bed we agreed on a formula to resolve the dispute.

Raghead: What was that then?

Monkey Hanger: She agreed to an improvement on quality of service and two less headaches a week.

Big Gus: Ahhh..... so ya let ya end down.

Monkey Hanger: No man, that was the problem, after three days of no nooky I couldn't get my end down.

Black Dave: But seven hundred quid for a pair of curtains....

Monkey Hanger: No man, it wunt the curtains that broke the bank. It was the thousand pounds for a new bed.

Raghead: Well ya not the only one who's on the bones this month. I'm skint.

Mary: It's been a real squeeze for me and Courtney as well. Things have been ever so tight.

Raghead: Have you tried Vaseline?

Fat Jeff: See what I mean Raghead. You've just done it again. Always lowering the tone of a serious conversation.

Raghead: All right, all right. I was only joking. Wiv a miserable lot like you, it's gonna be a long shift. Anyway what ya drawing?

[*Jeff shows Raghead what he has been drawing. It's a really crap drawing of a landscape that looks like it has been done by a child. He sits proudly waiting for an answer.*]

Fat Jeff: Took up art at night school on my days off. My tutor says I remind her of the surreal school.

[*The crew all look at the naff drawing*]

66

Monkey Hanger: She's right. What do ya say Raghead?

Raghead: It's definitely surreal. What is it?

Fat Jeff: Well can't ya tell? [*The crew all look at each other*] It's the south face of Mount Kilimanjairo.

Monkey Hanger:[*Sarcastic*] Oh yeah, can't ya see it Raghead?

Raghead: Looks like ya spilt ya coffee to me mate.

Fat Jeff: You've just got no eye for art Raghead, that's your problem. You wouldn't know a Van Gough from a Schubert.

Raghead: I know enough to know that Schubert was a musician.

Big Gus:[*Mocking*] Schubert. Mind you he was a bloody good banjo player.

Fat Jeff: You lot might take the piss, but my tutor says I've got real talent. And she should know, she puts on shows.

Black Dave: What, as a comedian?

Fat Jeff: My tutor says, art is just a matter of taste. Nothing is either bad or good. Everything is just a matter of opinion. Do you know last year a bloke in Hull sold a pile of bricks for nearly one hundred thousand pounds.

Monkey Hanger: I think my mate bought it actually. Was it a Barrett house?

Fat Jeff: Well you lot can laugh, but there's people making big bucks outa this type of thing these days. My tutor says it's only a matter of time before I get discovered. I just need to expose myself to the right people so they can have a good look at my portfolio.

Big Gus: Dirty bugger, you'll be getting yourself locked up.
[*They all laugh*]

Fat Jeff: Ya just can't have a serious conversation with you lot. I'm trying to get the conversation onto a higher plane, and all you lot can do is wallow in the gutter.

Raghead: Look what you've done now. You've upset his artistic temperament. He'll go all arty-farty on us in a minute.

Monkey Hanger: Yeah with a bit of luck he might cut off his ear. [*Raghead jokingly offers Jeff a bread knife*]

Raghead: Yeah we could frame it and put it in the Tate Modern.

Monkey hanger: You'll have to give it a title, all works of art have a title.

Raghead: Yeah what could we call it. How about "What's this Ear"?

> [*They all laugh. Malcolm who is engrossed in his Guardian suddenly interrupts the conversation.*]

Malcolm: Jeff's right about this art thing. I was watching The South Bank Show the other week. There was a bloke in it that made millions out of carving pigs and cows in half and putting them on show.

Fat Jeff: That's Damien Hurst that is. He's absolutely bloody loaded.

Raghead: Now I know ya lying. Nobody watches The South Bank Show.

Monkey Hanger: South Bank Show Eh Malc, bit of a culture vulture Eh.

Mary: Oooh yes, that Melvyn Bragg. My Courtney could just listen to him all night.

Raghead: In't he the bloke with that poncy haircut and a voice that sounds like somebody's got their finger up his arse.

Monkey Hanger: That's him.

Raghead: Ses it all then dunnit. It's bleedin geriatric hooray Henry's like him that turn real art upside down. I happened to be watching a programme one night and they had this African American bloke on, and you know what his artistic forty was? Sticking crucifixes and other religious stuff into old fish tanks and pissing in 'em.

Monkey Hanger: Bet he gets loads of publicity though.

Raghead: Course he did. That's the point. Wound up all the local religious fruitcakes big style. That's what he did it for. Get in the papers and there's a certain type rich tosser that will buy anything. All this modern art stuff is just is for people like Jeff who can't draw. I mean.....

[*Raghead picks up Fat Jeff's drawing and is scathing*]

Mount Kilimanjairo. Stuff like that ya see pinned to a nursery wall. Ya should send it in to Blue Peter.

Fat Jeff: Just a minute Raghead. Who are you to say what is art and what isn't? You're just a factory grunt with the imagination of a sub-normal monkey with brain damage. That bloke who carves up cows and stuff is one of the modern art world's most hailed figures. He's also stinking rich.

Raghead: It's all a bleedin con mate. That Melvyn Bragg gives 'em the publicity. Next thing ya know all the limp wrist London set are flocking to his shows. That Melvyn Bragg will be on commission mate. I bet he hasn't got half a pig hanging over his mantelpiece.

Monkey Hanger: Well that Damien Hurst can't be all daft can he? I mean if he doesn't sell his stuff, make hell of a Sunday roast.

Big Gus: Yeah then there's that bloke last year who won that Turner prize. Twenty grand for a bulb that switches on and off.

Raghead: Get away, ya having me on.

Fat Jeff: No that's straight up that is Raghead. I went to see it at the Tate Gallery in London. But they kicked me out.

Monkey Hanger: What for?

Fat Jeff: I thought the bulb was gone, so I switched the light off.

Black Dave: And he won twenty grand for a knackered light bulb?

Fat Jeff: I tell ya there's loads of money in this game.

69

Malcolm: [*Joking*] Maybe we should put on an exhibition of our own.

Fat Jeff: [*Revelation*] Eh that's not a bad idea. Bet we could make a fortune.

Monkey Hanger: Yeah, why not. All them toffs in London make loads out of it. Why not us? What do ya say Raghead?

Raghead: What a load of old bollocks. Them toffs in London make money 'cause they all know plenty of rich prats who will buy anything they say is art. Some of them people would hang turds on their living room wall if a Guardian arts critic said it was fashion.

Malcolm: I bet we could make a killing. We could all put on an exhibit. Eh I'll ring The Guardian.

Monkey Hanger: Well if the Guardian's coming I'm keeping me back to the wall.

Fat Jeff: Eh that's a brilliant idea. We might just start another fashion in the art of the northern working man.

Black Dave: They go for that type of pretentious crap in London.

Monkey Hanger: I bet we can get The Sun here if we tell 'em there's some tits in it. Come on Raghead.

Raghead: I'm having nowt to do with it I tell ya, you lot don't know the first thing about art. Art is about, blood, sweat, agony. It's about giving the world a glimpse of your inner-most soul and transferring the deep intellectual spirituality that has been torn from the inspirational flow of the creative juices and converted in a moment of the impetuous flicker of genius and transferred from the paintbrush to the canvas. You need only look at the renaissance period to see the trials, tribulations and continuing dark struggles of the classical artists, in contrast to, say, those of the Dada modernists. [*The crew all look in astonishment at Raghead*] And I'm sure Jeff would agree with me on that point.

[Fat Jeff coughs. He is clueless about what Raghead is going on about]

Fat Jeff: Well, er, yeah course I would.

Big Gus: Well it's the gold-fish I feel sorry for.

Monkey Hanger: Bloody 'ell ya just sound just like Melvyn Bragg.

[Raghead Laughs]

Fat Jeff: How do ya know all that then Raghead?

Raghead: Yeah good wannit. I just made it all up. But it fooled you lot dinnit? That's ya modern art mate.

Fat Jeff: Ah, you're just jealous Raghead, 'cause you haven't got no talent.

Raghead: Well you better come to this side of the table, 'cause ya ain't got none either.

Malcolm: Well at least Jeff is willing to put his talent to test like the rest of us. He's got more bottle than you.

Fat Jeff: That's right Malc. Raghead is just scared, 'cause he's scared he dunt win.

Raghead: It's got nowt to do with it. I 'ain't making a fool of myself. It dun't matter to Jeff 'cause everybody knows being a wanker is a full time profession for him, but I've got a reputation to keep.

[Big Gus gets up from the table and rolls up his newspaper]

Fat Jeff: Where you going?

Big Gus: If ya must know I'm going for a dump.

Fat Jeff: Well hurry up. We've all got a lot of work to do if we're putting on this exhibition.

Raghead: And don't flush the bog till Jeff's had a look. Ya never know it might just be a masterpiece.

[*A few days later — the canteen is more or less the same except the lads have each brought a painting they have done and they are exhibiting in the competition. Jeff and Malcolm have not brought in their exhibits yet. Mary and Black Dave are stood around near their exhibits.*

All the exhibits are covered up. The crew have also have tried to posh up the canteen in a tacky sort of way with a really tacky buffet. Monkey Hanger is dressed in his usual working clothes but has donned a black beret. Fat Jeff has put on an arty black velvet suit with a great big bow tie. Monkey Hanger is inspecting the buffet and tries to pinch some but Jeff is watching]

Fat Jeff: Eh you!! Keep ya dirty paws off. Our lass took all afternoon on that pate.

Monkey Hanger: Pate looks like potted meat to me.

Fat Jeff: Ya just like Raghead, no bloody culture. [*Jeff picks up one of the sandwiches*] Oh bloody 'ell they're beginning to curl. Put some plastic over them Monkey Hanger.

Monkey Hanger: I tell ya another thing. You've forgot the HP. Ya can't eat pork pie without a bit of HP on it.

Fat Jeff: Never mind that. They'll be in here in a minute and I haven't brought in me painting.

Monkey Hanger: Aye man, and where's Malc?

Fat Jeff: Trust him to be late.

[*At that precise moment Malcolm's head appears in the canteen doorway.*]

Malcolm: Eh Monkey Hanger give us a hand.

[*Monkey Hanger disappears through the door and suddenly a double bed is being pushed into the canteen*]

Fat Jeff: Bloody umbreago!! What the 'ell's that!!

Malcolm: It's all me own work.

Fat Jeff: Ya can't bring that in here.

Malcolm: It's me exhibit.

Fat Jeff: It's a bloody double bed. [*Malcolm starts to set it up by throwing the covers in an untidy heap and taking out a full ashtray and putting it at the side of the bed. He backs away and surveys his work of art, thumbing it like a real artist. He shakes his head and looks at Fat Jeff*]

Malcolm: I'm just not happy. I've got something missing.

Fat Jeff: Bloody right you have. Now get it moved.

Mary: Well I think it's quite chic! I like it Malcolm. Are the stains part of the artistic character?

Fat Jeff: That's not art!!

Monkey Hanger: Just a minute. You're the one who said art was a matter of opinion. Anyway where's your exhibit? They'll be here in a minute.

Fat Jeff: Oh bloody 'ell.

[*Jeff whips into the factory through another door and comes back carrying a big covered picture and puts it in on his stand. At that precise moment Raghead comes through the door into the canteen. He is dressed as normal in his working clothes. He is carrying a plastic bag with his packing up in. He looks around and scoffs.*]

Raghead: I tell ya if management get a whiff of this you lot will be for the high jump.

Fat Jeff: If all ya gonna do is put a damper on things sod off back in ya lab.

Raghead: I wouldn't miss this for the world and anyway I'm having me tea.

Fat Jeff: Well one sarcastic word from you when they come, [*Fat Jeff clenches his fist at Raghead.*] and I'll put this down ya throat.

73

[*A smirking Raghead goes over to the table and sits down*]

Raghead: I won't say a word!!

Fat Jeff: And leave the sandwiches alone. [*Raghead takes out a meat pie and unwraps it. He puts it on a nearby plate.*]

Raghead: Anybody seen the sauce?

Monkey Hanger: There ain't none. [*Raghead gets up.*]

Raghead: What sort of buffet is this, with no sauce. I've got some in the lab.

[*Raghead exits to the lab Monkey Hanger and Fat Jeff are stood by the table. The others are pottering about. Fat Jeff is getting nervous*]

Fat Jeff: I'm a bag of nerves. What time they due?

Monkey Hanger: Any minute now.

Fat Jeff: I'm bloody starving.

Monkey Hanger: Well have a sandwich then.

[*Fat Jeff looks at the spread and cringes. He picks up Raghead's pie*]

Fat Jeff: This looks nice.

Monkey Hanger: That's Raghead's. [*Fat Jeff takes a big bite and puts it back onto the plate just as two photographers come through the canteen door. He quickly chomps it up.*]

Fat Jeff: Oh shit it's the press. [*Monkey Hanger and Jeff go over to meet them*]

Photographer One: Is this the exhibition of manual workers' art?

Fat Jeff: You must be The Guardian?

Photographer Two: That's me. The Guardian Shoppers Weekly. Third largest free newspaper in the city. And remember, It's your newspaper.

Photographer One: How long's this gonna take? We've got a flower show at nine. What time are the big nobs coming?

Monkey Hanger: Don't worry mate you'll get all the pictures you want. We'll shout to you from the press gallery.

Photographer One: [*Sarcastic*] As long as we don't get caught in the scramble.

Photographer Two: Is that grub? I'm starving.

Monkey Hanger: Help yourself mate.

[*The two photographers go over to the buffet and start stuffing their faces. Raghead enters the canteen carrying a bottle of red sauce. He takes his seat back at the table. He is just about to get tucked into his pie when he sees that someone has taken a mouthful out of it. He is fuming. Monkey Hanger comes over.*]

Raghead: Have you had my pie?

Monkey Hanger: No it was Jeff.

[*Fat Jeff comes over. Raghead is fuming*]

Raghead: Are these your false teeth marks in my pie?!!

Fat Jeff: It was only one bite, now don't make a fuss Raghead, the press are watching. [*With that Raghead angrily throws his pie across the canteen at the wall were it sticks to the wall in a splatt and he storms out the canteen. Shot of the pie stuck to the wall. Fat Jeff starts sniggering to himself.*]

Fat Jeff: Well that's got rid of him.

[*At that precise moment a great entrance is made by the art expert Sir Jago Bagshot-Ponsenby Smythe and his female assistant Lady Nigella Arksworth-Fortescue.*

He is dressed stereotypically with a great black cloak and Fedora hat. His assistant, Lady Nigella, is also stereotypically dressed as you would expect for a "hooray Henry" type. The two photographers instantly drop their sandwiches and rush up to him and start snapping photographs. In true Prima Donna style Sir reluctantly poses for the cameras and swishes his cloak across his shoulders. Fat Jeff immediately goes over hand held out, Sir

Jago with a big smile goes straight past Fat Jeff and goes up to Monkey Hanger and gives him the full "Artistic Luvvy" greeting with kisses and all, much to Monkey Hanger's surprise.

He is followed with the greeting by Lady Nigella, only in this case Monkey Hanger is more than co-operative and enhances the greeting with a massive snog Fat Jeff rushes over to pull Monkey Hanger off.]

Fat Jeff: Give it a rest will ya.

[*Sir Jago assumes that Monkey Hanger is in charge and addresses him as such totally ignoring Fat Jeff.*]

Sir Jago: So you are the personage responsible for this artistic endeavour?

[*Fat Jeff interrupts with a smile*]

Fat Jeff: No that would be me.

[*Sir Jago is not impressed and looks down his nose at Fat Jeff*]

Sir Jago: My apologies I thought you were the bouncer. [*At this point photographer one interrupts*]

Photographer One: Could we have a few more pictures Sir Jago and perhaps a few words.

Sir Jago: All in good time gentlemen, all in good time. Oh how tiresome to be constantly under the public eye.

Fat Jeff: I know just how you feel Sir Jago. I never had the press off my doorstep after they caught my next door neighbour fiddling the Social.

Photographer Two: If I could just ask you Sir Jago, did you think the Judge's comments at your recent trial concerning the male stripper and the goat were relevant?

[*At that point Fat Jeff interrupts*]

Fat Jeff: Well I think that is a good moment for Sir Jago to move on to the exhibits.

[Fat Jeff points Sir Jago in the direction of the crew waiting with their covered exhibits. Monkey Hanger lags behind and whispers to the photographers]

Monkey Hanger: What's that about a male stripper and a goat?

[Suddenly Sir Jago stops dead in his tracks as his eye is caught by what he thinks is an exhibit.]

Sir Jago: Good God!! Magnificent!!

Fat Jeff: What is?

Sir Jago: Nigella just look at the enigmatic arrangement. It is of course typical of the classical artesian style.

[Fat Jeff is a bit bemused since Sir Jago is looking at the coat rack.]

Lady Nigella: Yes, yes. There is definitely something sexual.

Fat Jeff: *[Staring hard]* There is?!!

Sir Jago: What do you call it?

Fat Jeff: A coat rack.

Sir Jago: A coat rack. Such simplicity of name is indeed a mark of brilliance. If this is an example of the standard of work, this indeed is going to be a pleasure of the senses. Lead on!!

[Next on the list is Malcolm's dirty bed. Malcolm is stood next to his "exhibit" with a proud gormless smile. Sir Jago is aghast. He prances around the exhibit artistically thumbing and eyeing it]

Sir Jago: Now this is really saying something, but I can't make it out.

Monkey Hanger: That's because it's humming.

Sir Jago: Nigella!! Your thoughts.....

Lady Nigella: Yes, yes. I see it. It's definitely something sexual.

Sir Jago: There's just something missing.

Malcolm: That's what I thought….. Just a minute!! I know!!!

[*Suddenly Malcolm is struck with inspiration. He kicks off his shoes, takes off his trousers, and with his back to the camera removes his underpants and throws them artistically on the bed. Shot from back of Malcolm of Sir Jago*]

Sir Jago: That's it! What a magnificent piece!!

[*Fat Jeff whispers to Monkey Hanger.*]

Fat Jeff: Yeah, but where's he looking?

Sir Jago: My boy with a sculpture like that, your future is assured.

[*Fat Jeff picks Malcolm's underpants off the bed with two fingers and throws them at a smiling Malcolm.*]

Fat Jeff: Well ya can get ya piece covered up now. [*They move onto to Black Dave with his covered piece.*]

Sir Jago: Ah yes, the native art form. The symbolism cries out the pain of the suffering of the dark continent. [*Sir Jago pats Black Dave on the shoulder.*] Keep up the good work my boy.

[*Sir Jago moves on to Big Gus and his covered exhibit*]

Black Dave: [*To Fat Jeff*] Brilliant that bloke. Saw all that and I didn't even take the cover off.

[*Big Gus suddenly pulls the cover off his exhibit. It is a fish tank with a picture of the Pope in it. It is full of a liquid, Shot of Fat Jeff looking at Big Gus.*]

Fat Gus: Ya didn't?!!

Big Gus: Took me four days to fill it.

Sir Jago: Mmmmm…. interesting.

Big Gus: Oh just a minute. [*He throws a switch at the side and a light starts to go on and off inside the tank.*]

Sir Jago: I am simply astounded by the nuance of the piece. Particularly I am drawn to the delicate way the colours flaunt themselves around the delicate tone of the liquid.[*Sir Jago turns to Fat Jeff.*] It really is bliss.

Fat Jeff: I knew you'd smell it.

Sir Jago: Nigella? [*Nigella does her artistic "dance" before giving her opinion.*]

Lady Nigella: There's definitely something sexual here.

[*Fat Jeff whispers to Monkey Hanger next to him.*]

Fat Jeff: There's definitely something not right about that girl.

Monkey Hanger: Well ya know what these Lady aristocrats are like. She's probably worn out the stable lad and not had a good humping for weeks.

[*Sir Jago is still engrossed in Big Gus's sculpture.*]

Sir Jago: Nigella, this man could be another Warhole. Onward!!

[*Sir Jago moves to the next exhibit. It is Fat Jeff's. Monkey Hanger whispers to Fat Jeff*]

Monkey Hanger: Did he say Warhole or arsehole?

[*Sneaky smile to Monkey Hanger.*]

Fat Jeff: This'll knock him out.

[*Fat Jeff pauses before unveiling his exhibit, as if teasing those watching.*]

Sir Jago: Come, come my good man. Your audience is breathless with anticipation.

[*Fat Jeff suddenly wafts the cover away from his painting to unveil what any ordinary person would call a stunning landscape. But Sir Jago is totally unimpressed and his expression is totally disdainful. Fat Jeff is smiling*]

Sir Jago: Eeeeeeeh!! Good grief!! By the Gods I've never seen anything like it.

Fat Jeff: [*Still Smiling*] I knew you'd be impressed.

Sir Jago: [*Outraged*] Impressed!! Impressed!! You Sir!! Are a cad!! A Charlatan!! My senses have just been assaulted by this visual outrage. How dare you Sir aspire to the audacity to bestow this abomination under such a term as art. [*Fat Jeff is confused.*]

Fat Jeff: Just a bloody minute! Outrage, abomination? [*Fat Jeff points to Malcolm's bed and Big Gus's fish tank*] You call that art, and have the cheek to call my painting an outrage. What do you think Monkey Hanger?

[*Monkey Hanger goes all arty and gives Lady Nigella a wink.*]

Monkey Hanger: There's definitely something sexual !!

Sir Jago: You Sir are a cheat!!

Fat Jeff: What do you mean a cheat? [*Sir Jago looks behind the painting and pulls out a box. It is clearly marked. "PAINTING BY NUMBERS"*]

Malcolm: You cheat!!

Big Gus: Bloody cheek. Raghead was right about you. No bleedin' talent.

Fat Jeff: But, but, it's still art?

Sir Jago: Art!! You Sir know nothing about art!! Art is about, blood,sweat, agony. It's about giving the world a glimpse of your inner most soul.

Fat Jeff: Oh yeah, oh yeah. Well where have I heard those words before and he's a bloody conman an 'all.

[*At that moment Raghead enters the canteen. Sir Jago goes all limp at Fat Jeff's insult.*]

Sir Jago: I've never been so insulted in my life.

Fat Jeff: Well try getting out more.

Raghead: What's up wiv Quenten Crisp then? [*Monkey Hanger laughing.*]

Monkey Hanger: Caught Fat Jeff cheating.

Sir Jago: Nigella let us take our leave of this moron.

[*Outraged Sir Jago minces towards the canteen door. Suddenly he stops dead in his tracks and is almost in a trance as he stares at the wall. We do not see what he is looking at. Sir Jago is almost breathless when he speaks*]

Sir Jago: Nigella!! Nigella!! Have you ever seen anything like it?

[*Lady Nigella goes into a similar trance like state.*]

Lady Nigella: Sheer genius.

Sir Jago: What is this called?

Monkey Hanger: That's Raghead's Pie.

[*Shot of Raghead's Pie stuck to the wall.*]

Sir Jago: [*To himself*] Raghead's Pies. Even the title is almost artesian poetry.

[*The crew all gather round it and stare.*]

Fat Jeff: It does? [*Raghead sees his opportunity.*]

Raghead: I'm sure you can see that the interpretation is eurythmic in style.

Sir Jago: Absolutely. Can you tell us anymore?

Raghead: Well it's best steak and kidney.

Sir Jago: My good man. I must have it. Nigella the cheque book. [*Nigella gets out the cheque book and gives it to Sir Jago*] Name your price Sir?

[*Raghead is suddenly stuck for words.*]

Monkey Hanger: Go on Raghead, name ya price.

Raghead: Fifty'll be alright I suppose.

[*Sir Jago starts to write out the cheque.*]

Sir Jago: Fifty thousand pounds only. [*The crew are all stunned*]

Fat Jeff: Fifty grand for that!!

[*Sir Jago snaps off the cheque and hands it to Raghead*]

Sir Jaygo: Get your coat my boy.

Raghead: Where we going?

Sir Jago: My boy, the world awaits your genius. New York awaits!!

[*The photographers have pushed their way into the canteen and snap some posing photographs. Raghead is suddenly aware of Lady Nigella posing next to him and cheekily puts his arm around her*] Now let us take our leave of this place and depart this nest of Philistines.

[*They all turn and Sir Jago, Raghead with arm still around Lady Nigella go out the door. Monkey Hanger shouts after Raghead*]

Monkey Hanger: But Raghead, what are you gonna do!!?

[*Raghead turns his head with a big grin and his arm slips down and squeezes Lady Nigella's backside. Lady Nigella turns round to look at Monkey Hanger.*]

Lady Nigella: Definitely something sexual!!

[*All the rest of the lads wear stunned expressions.*]

THE PHANTOM PEBBLE DASHER

Character that appears in this episode only: Inspector Arnwee Le Dung (A French private detective)

The action takes place in the canteen/smoke room and female toilets for office staff.

We open with a shot of a door. The door is marked "Office Staff Only. Female Toilets"

Inside one of the cubicles inside the toilet Raghead is asleep. The toilet is in semi-darkness. Raghead's four front false teeth are resting on the toilet roll holder. He is sat on the toilet giving it loads of Z's and snoring his head off. He has a comfortable pillow that he is resting his head on. He is in dreamland. All is silent in the toilet. Someone enters the toilet and goes into the cubicle next to where Raghead is asleep. Raghead slowly opens his eyes as he realises he is not alone. He hears a loud rasping splatter from the customer next-door bringing Raghead wide-awake. He cringes his face as the smell comes into the cubicle. He bangs on the wall to protest

Raghead: Do you bleedin'mind there's people trying to sleep in here.

[*We hear more loud rasping rumbles from next door. Raghead again bangs on the toilet wall and cringes with the smell.*]

Raghead: You should get medical help mate, smells like something crawled up ya and died. [*There is no reply. Raghead looks worried. He looks under the cubicle wall and sees an absolutely massive pair of dirty feet.*] Jeff, is that you? [*There is no reply.*] Gus? ......Come on stop messing about. [*There is no reply. Raghead looks more worried. He puts his teeth in and gets up.*] Monkey Hanger?!!

[*Suddenly there is a loud evil echoing laugh from the cubicle next door. Raghead eyes open wide with fear. He hears the toilet door next-door open. He rushes out of the toilet only to see the main toilet door closing.*

He creeps over to the main light and turns it on. He then stealthily creeps over to the cubicle that has just been speedily vacated by the mystery visitor and carefully pushes open the door. He walks into the cubicle and looks into the toilet pan. He is horrified.]

Raghead: Eeeeeeeh!!!!

[*Meanwhile back in the canteen/smoke room Mary, Black Dave and Malcolm are sitting around. As usual the table is strewn with clutter, dirty cups, ashtrays etc. Mary and Black Dave are reading. Malcolm is on his feet and is taking out a cake from his packing up bag. He plonks it in the middle of the table. It looks nice.*]

Mary: Spoiling yourself Malcolm?

Malcolm: Thought I'd bring a treat in for the shift. I get fed up of sandwiches and soup.

Black Dave: I know what you mean mate. Shifts and junk food are the worst thing for ya body clock. Gives me the runs something terrible.

Mary: Well what I try do is have a wholesome meal before I come to work. Tonight Courtney cooked me a lovely Vindaloo. In fact I've brought some in if anyone wants some?

Black Dave: Vindaloo!! No thanks mate. Bet you'll pay for that later on.

Malcolm: Don't worry. It won't go to waste Raghead'll have it.

Mary: I don't where he puts it. Like a bloody gannet he is.

[*At that moment Raghead enters the canteen in a panic.*]

Malcolm: Mention the devil and he appears. Mary's got some free grub going Raghead.

Raghead: Never mind that!! Who's the bleedin' joker then?

Malcolm: What ya on about Raghead?

[*Raghead is accusing.*]

Raghead: Some dirty gitt has just done a hit and run in the women's bogs downstairs. Scared the living daylights outa me, and he's left a right mess in there. Stunk me outa the place.

Mary: Well we've been in here all night. So don't go pointing the finger in this direction. Anyway what were you doing in there? Sleeping I suppose.

Raghead: Well if ya knew, why'd ya ask? Has he been in here all night Malcolm?

Mary: I resent that remark. You want some proof before ya go accusing people.

Malcolm: He's been in here all night wiv me and Dave.

Black Dave: That's right.

Malcolm: You 'aint half ungrateful Raghead. Mary's brought Vindaloo for the shift.

[*Raghead is more suspicious,*]

Raghead: Vindaloo eh.

[*He walks over to Mary and has a sniff around.*]

Mary: Do you mind!!

Raghead: Just checking I'll never forget that smell.

[*At that point Big Gus comes through the factory door with Fat Jeff. They look serious. Big Gus is carrying a dirty toilet brush and Fat Jeff a plunger and they are both wearing Wellingtons. They stand there staring at those already in the canteen. Raghead looks at them both and cringes at the smell*]

Raghead: Phew!! What the bleedin 'ell have you two been up to?

[*Fat Jeff addresses them seriously.*]

85

Fat Jeff: I'm warning all of you lot. Who ever is doing it had better stop!!

Malcolm: What?!!

Big Gus: I've just spent nearly an hour in the bog in there.

Malcolm: Have ya seen a doctor?

Big Gus: Not using 'em!! Cleaning and unblocking 'em. Every bog in place has been abused.

Fat Jeff: Bloody 'orrible it was.

Raghead: That's just happened down stairs in the women's office bogs.

Fat Jeff: Oh no!! Not the office bogs again. The MD's fuming about the state the executive bogs were left in.

[*At that moment Monkey Hanger comes into the canteen. He is not happy.*]

Monkey Hanger: [*North east accent*] This place is a bloody disgrace. Have ya seen the state of the bogs over there? Which one of you dirty sods can't use a toilet brush? [*Monkey Hanger sees Big Gus holding the toilet brush.*] Oh yes, I see you've caught the culprit then Jeff. You want to be ashamed of ya self. Ya mucky sod!!

Big Gus: Don't bloody look at me.

Monkey Hanger: Well what ya carrying that for? Don't tell me it's ya toothbrush.

Big Gus: I've bin bloody cleaning up the mess in the factory bogs.

Monkey Hanger: What!! In there as well?!!

Raghead: And the office bogs!! I've just had a right scare in there.

Monkey Hanger: Who is it then?

Raghead: I didn't get a look. Who ever it is moved bloody fast.

Dropped his guts and ran like the wind. It was all over in a splash.

Fat Jeff: We've only got your word for that.

[*Big Gus points at Raghead with the toilet brush.*]

Big Gus: Yeah, that's right.

[*Big Gus goes towards Raghead. He is still pointing the toilet brush at him. Big Gus looks angry. Raghead begins to back away.*]

Raghead: Don't point ya brush at me mate.

Big Gus: I'm warning you Raghead, I've got better things to do with my time than clean up after you.[*Big Gus is poking Raghead in the shoulder with the toilet brush.*] If I find out it's you.....

[*Fat Jeff intervenes before things get out of hand.*]

Fat Jeff: Calm down Gus. Just put ya tools down a minute and let's be rational about this.

Mary: Yes but Gus has got a point. We do only have your word.

Malcolm: Yeah, we've all got alibis.

[*Everybody is looking at Raghead.*]

Raghead: Just a minute!! What about Monkey Hanger? He hasn't got an alibi.

Monkey Hanger: I've bin in the control room man.

Fat Jeff: Yeah, but we've only got your word for that as well. Either of you two could be The Phantom.

Monkey Hanger: What do you mean, The Phantom?

[*At that precise moment a French voice echoes across the canteen.*]

"EVERYBODY!! STAY WHERE YOU ARE!!"

[*Everyone is totally shocked as a Frenchman in a Trilby hat and wearing a white Mackintosh comes into the canteen. He lights his pipe. This Frenchman has a really strong French accent*]

Fat Jeff: Bloody Umbreago!! Who are you?

Frenchman: I am Arnwee Le Dung. I have been employed by your company to get to the bottom of this mess.

Fat Jeff: Just a minute. I haven't been told anything about this.

Frenchman: Both I and your MD thought it best I remain under-cover. I have been listening to your conversation. I thought it best if I expose myself now.[*The Frenchman walks over to Fat Jeff.*] And I think you are right.

Fat Jeff: What do you mean?

Frenchman: There is a Phantom loose in this factory.

Raghead: I'll second that. He's definitely loose.

Fat Jeff: You mean?

Frenchman: Yes, this is a classic case. All the signs are there. What we 'ave 'ere Gentlemen, is a serial Phantom Pebble Dasherrr at large in this factory. And I am here to help flush him out.

Monkey Hanger: But ya can't think it's any of us?

Frenchman: Everyone is under suspicion. Now you will all sit down and do as I say.

[*The crew all stare at each other. Later they are all sat round the canteen table. The Frenchman is stood up still puffing on his pipe.*]

Frenchman: Someone in this room is the Phantom Pebble Dasher.

Big Gus: Well it in't me!!

Mary: Or me!!

Black Dave: Don't look at me.

Fat Jeff: This whole thing stinks. We've all got alibis except Raghead and Monkey Hanger.

[*The Frenchman looks in Raghead's direction.*]

Frenchman: Ah yes, Raghead.

Raghead: What ya looking at me like that for?

Frenchman: You seem to be the only one who has had a close encounter with the Phantom.

Raghead: Well I didn't see him? It all happened so quickly.

Frenchman: Would you know him if you smelt him again?

Raghead: I never forget that smell as long as I live. Horrible it was.

Frenchman: And you remember nothing else?

Raghead: Oh yeah, there was this evil laugh, made ya blood run cold it did. Oh yeah, I looked under the door and there were these enormous dirty feet. At first I thought it was Jeff.

Fat Jeff: Don't bring me into this. I don't use the women's bogs.

Frenchman: Ah so that brings us to the question of what you were doing in the women's toilets?

Malcolm: Oh Raghead's always in there.

Frenchman: Ahhh, is he now?

[Raghead goes all coy.]

Raghead: Well I was, ere passing, that's right. I was passing and I went in to check.

Frenchman: Check what?

Raghead: I heard a noise.

Frenchman: And tell me, do you always look under doors in women's toilets?

Raghead: It wasn't like that!!

Fat Jeff: I've always had me doubts about you Raghead.

Malcolm: Eeeeh looking under toilet doors. You're a perv Raghead.

Frenchman: So what happened then?

Raghead: It's a bit of a blur. I remember there was this evil laugh.

Frenchman: And then?

Raghead: He was gone. All I saw was his calling card.

Frenchman: So you did not challenge him?

Raghead: Bloody 'ell ya kidding after I looked in, there was no way I could have beaten that.

Frenchman: But you are forgetting something important are you not?

Raghead: I can't think what?

Frenchman: The fumble of the toilet roll?

Raghead: That's right. He must have moved so fast he forgot to clean his eye out.

[*The Frenchman smiles with satisfaction.*]

Frenchman: Exactly. Who ever The Phantom Pebble Dasher is, has probably left the evidence behind. It is therefore a simple process of elimination.

Fat Jeff: I'm not sure I like the sound of this.

Monkey Hanger: What ya mean, drop our kegs like?

Mary: What for!! What's that going to prove?

Malcolm: It's like taking your finger prints innit. He just wants to look at all probables.

Mary: Well he's not looking at my probables.

Frenchman: I think at this point perhaps we pause and take stock of the situation.

[*The Frenchman goes to a nearby board and picks up a marker pen. The board is not facing the crew who are sat down at the table.*]

Frenchman: Let's see what we have so far. Now Raghead, you thought it was Jeff?

Fat Jeff: Eh now just a bleedin' minute.

Frenchman: We are just gathering facts at the moment mon juer. You are no more a suspect at this stage anyone else. So..

[*The Frenchman writes down the clue on the board.*]

Frenchman: What else do we know about the Dasherrrr?

Big Gus: He's been on every bog in the place.

[*The Frenchman writes down another clue.*]

Frenchman: Correct.

Monkey Hanger: Oh the stink!!

[*The Frenchman writes down another clue on the board.*]

Raghead: Oh the evil laugh, something horrible it was.

Frenchman: Good, Good, Good, [*More clues are written down by the Frenchman.*] Something horrible!!

[*The Frenchman stands back and looks at his clue board.*]

Monkey Hanger: Come on then man lets have a look what we've got?

[*The Frenchman turns the clue board round to face the crew. It reads: "JEFF ON THE BOG STINKS SOMETHING HORRIBLE"*]

Monkey Hanger: Well that was a useful exercise.

Raghead: Oh this is getting us nowhere. We all know the Phantom has to be one of us in this room. It's simple enough to find out.

Fat Jeff: Go on then Sherlock. How?

Raghead: I know it isn't me. Malc, Mary and Black Dave have got each other for alibis. And Big Gus was with you. So it has to be Monkey Hanger.

Monkey Hanger: Oh wait a minute man. I know it wasn't me. So that only leaves……..

[*All the crew suddenly turn their eyes towards the Frenchman.*]

Frenchman: Sacra Blur!!

Fat Jeff: Yeah just a minute. You could be anybody.

Frenchman: I am employed by your company.

Raghead: We've only got your word for that. I mean, how do we know you are, who you say you are? You could be Jack The Shitter for all we know?

Frenchman: That is ridiculous mon.

Fat Jeff: Yeah, you drop ya kegs. Prove you're not the The Phantom Pebble Dasher?

Frenchman: If you insist mon am me. A Frenchman is always happy to get his pants down.

[*The Frenchman pulls up his Mackintosh, drop his kegs and bends over a nearby table. He is wearing immaculate white underpants.*]

Raghead: Somebody hold onto Mary.

Fenchman: You have your proof now!

[*The crew all groan with disappointment. The Frenchman pulls up his kegs and pulls down his Mackintosh.*]

Now Gentlemen, the balls is in your court?

Fat Jeff: This is bloody undignified this is. I 'aint getting me kegs off.

Frenchman: Perhaps you have something to hide inside your pants?

Fat Jeff: I've got an alibi remember.

Frenchman: So you have. Mr Gus, you can confirm that Jeff was with you all night?

Big Gus: Well yes most of the time. He did go off somewhere for a few minutes.

Raghead: So he wasn't with you all night then!! Ya left that bit out dint ya. Bloody quick trying to put the blame on me.

Frenchman: And about what time was it that Mosuir Jeff left?

Big Gus: Just before we came into the canteen about eight. He was gone about ten minutes.

Raghead: That's exactly the time I bumped into the Dasher.

Fat Jeff: Now just a bloody minute. This all proves nothing. It takes at least fives minutes to get to the office toilets from where I was in the factory.

Frenchman: But time enough. And Dasherrrs are known for their speed.

Raghead: Well carrying that lot, they have to be.

Frenchman: Now Mosuir Jeff perhaps there is something else you are not telling us?

Fat Jeff: I don't know what you're talking about.

Monkey Hanger: Oh eye what's going on here? Come Jeff spill the beans.

Frenchman: Then let me refresh your memory. September 8th 1982. [*The Frenchman pulls a note book from his pocket.*] You were fined fifty pounds by Bournemouth Magistrates. For an act of indecency which took place at the Dog and Duck public house.

Raghead: You dirty bugger, ya kept that one quiet.

Fat Jeff: But that was years ago. Ya can't hold that against me. It was a night out with the lads. I'd had about sixteen pints of Newcastle brown and mushy peas. Everybody's got skeletons in the cupboard.

[*The Frenchman continues to read his note book.*]

Frenchman: And what about Salford October 7th 1992?

Monkey Hanger: Skeletons in the cupboard!! You've got a bloody graveyard in there mate.

Fat Jeff: Look I'm cured now. I tell ya I'm not the Phantom.

Frenchman: Then prove it.

Fat Jeff: Alright, alright.

[*Fat Jeff stands up drops his kegs and displays his clean underpants.*] See I told ya. Bloody satisfied now!!

Malcolm: But that dunt prove nowt with your record.

Fat Jeff: Clever bugger you are, well let's have a look at yours?

[*Fat Jeff makes a grabs at Malcolm's overall trousers.*]

Malcolm: Ere get off!!

Fat Jeff: Just a minute.!! Let's have a look at the label? [*Fat Jeff reads the tag at the back of the trousers.*] Ya thieving sod. These are my spare trousers. You've been in my Locker.

[*Malcolm is struggling with Jeff.*]

Malcolm: No I haven't, I got them out the dirty laundry after I ran out.

Raghead: Bloody 'ell wearing Jeff's dirty clothes. You've got some mucky habits you have.

Fat Jeff: Well come on! Let's have a look then!!

[*Fat Jeff is still tugging at his trousers. He looks down the back and gets a surprise.*]

Fat Jeff: You 'ain't got non on!!

Monkey Hanger: Oh got rid of the evidence eh?

Malcolm: No if ya must know I don't wear 'em. My mum ses it's more hygienic with all the sweating and stuff round the three piece suite.

Raghead: [*Laughing*] Except for Jeff, ehhhhhhhhhhh.

94

Fat Jeff: Never mind laughing Raghead, it's your turn.

Raghead: Well I'm not showing me skiddies for anybody.

Big Gus: Me neither. It's bleedin' undignified it is.

Monkey Hanger: You can't come in here and just order us to drop our kegs. Ya not in Frogland now. This is Great Britain mate. No one makes a fool of us British, as your Napoleon discovered after Wellington kicked his head in at Waterloo.

Frenchman: Your insults monjur will not destract me from my duty.

Someone in this room is The Phantom Pebble Dasher. And until we find out who he is, no one moves.

Raghead: But who's gonna do my work?

Fat Jeff: Well it's never bothered you for fifteen years. Why worry now.

Frenchman: It is only a matter of time before The Dasher has to show himself again.

Big Gus: What do you mean?

Frenchman: If one of you is The Dasher, then sooner or later, he will have to go.

Monkey Hanger: Yeah that's right.

Frenchman: And I will be waiting to get the drop on him.

Raghead: Just make sure he doesn't get the drop on you first.

Fat Jeff: So we're just gonna sit here and wait till the Dasher shows his hand?

Black Dave: But that could take all night.

[*The Frenchman smiles, sits down and puffs on his pipe.*]

Frenchman: I think not. I have been involved in cases like this before. Psychological profiles of serial Phantom Pebble Dashers show that sooner or later there is an irresistable urge for Dashers to committ another unspeakable act of anal felony. In France I am regarded as a leading authority on the subject. Perhaps you might have read the paper I wrote for The Vienna Institute?

Fat Jeff: You know I don't think I did. What about you Raghead?

Raghead: Damn! I must have missed it.

Monkey Hanger: So this isn't your first case of this type then?

Frenchman: No, no. I have hunted Pebble Dashers in many countries.

Fat Jeff: So Pebble Dashers are no respectors of national borders?

Frenchman: They are an international scourge. The internet now provides them with access to other Pebble Dashers all over the globe. There are rumours of Pebble Dasher cells at the highest levels of government.

Raghead: What you mean they might be in the government like?

Frenchman: It is a fact that that your own number 10 has been infiltrated by several Pebble Dashers.

Malcolm: Bloody 'ell Pebble Dashers in number 10.

Raghead: Shouldn't bother that lot, they're used to making a mess they won't clean up.

Fat Jeff: This sounds like quite a specialist field then hunting Pebble Dashers.

Frenchman: Mon dur ! Psychological profiling of The Pebble Dasher reveals usually a deranged beast who has little consideration for his fellow man. Many are loners.

Raghead: Never!!

Frenchman: There are many types of Pebble Dashers. In this particular case, we seem to dealing with a particularly evil type. A Phantom Pebble Dasher. Someone who cares little about suspicion falling on his fellow workers. He is very dangerous and must not be approached.

Fat Jeff: Especially when crouching eh?

Big Gus: But all this talk doesn't get us anywhere. We still don't know who it is.

[*The Frenchman cleverly smiles.*]

Frenchman: Indeed. But plans are already afoot. If all goes well we will have the Dasher in our hands by morning.

Fat Jeff: But how?

[*The Frenchman takes out something that looks like a mobile phone.*]

Frenchman: With this box of tricks. I should warn all of you. All the toilets are alarmed. As soon as anyone enters any of them, an alarm will sound on this machine. And my men outside will surround the place, and the Dasher will be taken into custody.

Malcolm: But what if one of us needs to go?

Big Gus: Yeah, we can't sit here all night!!

Frenchman: No one will move!! Eventually the Dasher will be forced to show himself, and we will be waiting.

Raghead: Well if that's the case. We might as well get the grub on. Whose cake is this?

Malcolm: Mine.

Monkey Hanger: Well don't just sit there get a knife.

Raghead: Never mind that, who needs a knife.

[*Raghead pulls out his four front false teeth and uses them to cut the cake.*]

Monkey Hanger: Ya dirty bugger. I hope ya washed your hands.

Raghead: Come on then Mary get that grub ya brought.

Fat Jeff: I'm bleedin starvin. I hope there's enough for all of us.

[*All the shift tuck in and are soon totally full*]

Fat Jeff: Bloody umbreago, that was lovely. I'm bloody bursting.

[*The lads round the table are in the same state of over eating.*]

Big Gus: By 'ell that Courtney of yours cooks a mean Vindaloo.

[*Raghead leans forward and breaks winds.*]

Raghead: Better out than in as my old gran used to say.

Fat Jeff: That depends where ya sitting.

[*Monkey Hanger also breaks wind*]

Monkey Hanger: Not quite tortoise head.

[*Big Gus then gives a big blast of breaking wind.*]

Big Gus: Bloody 'ell excuse me, almost followed through there.

[*Malcolm is wafting away the smell with his hand.*]

Malcolm: Smells like ya did from here.

[*Mary then also gives off a petit fart. The crew all look at him*]

Mary: What you looking at me like that for? I'm only human.

Raghead: I don't know about you lot but I'm bloody knackered.

[*The crew all suddenly start to stretch and yawn, with all of them going to sleep including the Frenchman. Suddenly the alarm goes off in the Frenchman's pocket and he wakes up with a jerk. The canteen is empty. The crew have gone.*]

Frenchman: Sacra Blur!!

[*He rushes for the door and dashes across to the executive toilets, shoving open the toilet door. Inside the very smart office toilets as the Frenchman enters he is taken aback by the smell. The place is filled with the sound of breaking wind from inside the cubicles. All the cubicles are engaged.*

The Frenchman puts a handkerchief over his mouth and looks under each toilet door in turn. We see one by one a pair of

98

working boot's until the Frenchman comes to the last cubicle and there is a pair of dirty great feet inside. The Frenchman gets too close to the bottom of the door for a closer look, his head almost going under the door. Suddenly a hand grabs him and we see him being dragged under the toilet door. The Frenchman is screaming as he is dragged under. We hear a lot of splutter and splatter and then the Frenchman's screams are silent.]

Fat Jeff: What was that noise? Like someone screaming.

Raghead: Didn't hear nowt, did you Mary?

Mary: I had my mind on other things. That's the thing about Vindaloo. Ghandi's revenge.

[*One by one the crew merge from the cubicle until they are all out barring one cubicle, and Monkey Hanger is missing. They are all washing their hands. The outside toilet door closes. One cubicle is still engaged. We hear an evil laugh. A lock clicks and Monkey Hanger comes out of the cubicle. He leaves behind a pair of legs sticking out of the toilet pan. They are the Frenchman's.*]